Talk About the Cover

Frogs

Sitting on a lily pad,

Eating **BUGS** is not too bad.

Hopping, splashing in the **SUN**,

Frogs can have a lot of FUN.

How high can YOU hop?

Moving into English

Authors

Alma Flor Ada • F. Isabel Campoy • Yolanda N. Padrón • Nancy Roser

Harcourt

Orlando   Austin   Chicago   New York   Toronto   London   San Diego

Visit *The Learning Site!*
www.harcourtschool.com

UNIT
1
SELF-DISCOVERY

CONTENTS

Self-Discovery

Review Vocabulary with a Play
★ STORIES ON STAGE ★

Working Together

Review Vocabulary with a Play
STORIES ON STAGE

UNIT
3
GROWTH AND CHANGE

CONTENTS

Growth and Change

Review Vocabulary with a Play
★ STORIES ON STAGE ★

4

CONTENTS

Creativity

Unit Review

CONTENTS

Communities

Review Vocabulary with a Play
★ STORIES ON STAGE ★

CONTENTS

Explorations

Review Vocabulary with a Play
★ STORIES ON STAGE ★

Use What You Know

▪ When You Read and Write

I know that an elephant is big. **Gigantic** might mean the same as **big**. I can use the word **gigantic** when I write about something big.

▪ When You Listen and Speak

My mom is a police officer. I know what she does. I know what Officer Sam is talking about. I can tell people about police officers.

Find Help

■ When You Read and Write

- I can look in a **dictionary**.
- I can ask a **friend**.
- I can ask my **teacher**.

dictionary

friend

teacher

■ When You Listen and Speak

- I can raise my hand and ask a question.
- I can write a question to ask later.

Make Connections

■ When You Read and Write

I live in a city.

I read a book about farms.

I can write about how a city and a farm are alike and different.

The city is busy. The farm is quiet.

■ When You Listen and Speak

The word **frigid** sounds like **refrigerator**. A refrigerator keeps things cold. I think **frigid** means "cold." I can use the word **frigid** when I talk about something cold.

Picture It

■ When You Read and Listen

I make a picture in my mind. It helps me understand what I read or hear.

The hummingbird is smaller than the flower.

■ When You Write and Speak

I make a picture in my mind.

I can write about the picture.

I can talk about the picture.

Look for Patterns

■ When You Read and Listen

What does **celery** mean? I see a pattern. Each sentence has a vegetable. Celery must be a vegetable!

I have **lettuce**.

I have **carrots**.

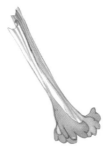

I have **celery**.

■ When You Write and Speak

I can teach my sister to tie her shoes. I will tell her the steps. I will say, "First, next, and last." I can write the steps so she will always remember them.

Set a Purpose

■ When You Read and Listen

I can ask myself

- What am I reading?
- Who is talking?
- What do I want to know?

■ When You Write and Speak

I can ask myself

- Who will read what I write?
- Who is listening to me?
- What do I want people to know?

SING ALONG

The More I Learn About Me

The more I learn about me,

About me, about me,

The more I learn about me,

The happier I will be.

 Sing to the tune of
"Did You Ever See a Lassie?"

15

Word Clues

As you read, you will find words you do not know. **Word clues** can help you understand a new word. Read the other words and sentences around the new word. Think about the word order in the sentence.

Read these sentences.

Tony darted into the kitchen.

**"Slow down!" Mom said.
"Don't run in the house."**

To figure out the word **darted**, look at these word clues.

Word Clues	
Other Words and Sentences	Mom tells Tony to slow down.
Word Order	**Darted** is something that Tony does to get into the kitchen.

Word clues help you figure out that **darted** means "moved quickly."

▶ Read these sentences.

Tony was happy. He was going on a journey with his family. He knew this trip would be fun.

Copy this chart. Add the word clues that helped you figure out the meaning of the word **journey**.

Word Clues	
Other Words and Sentences	.
Word Order	

LESSON 1

Sometimes ▼

VOCABULARY

happy

sad

hot

cold

red

blue

The boy was **happy** when he got a puppy.

I am **sad** when my friends go home.
It makes me feel **blue**.

Snow is **cold**, so we wear lots of clothes.

My mom is **hot** after she runs.

This girl's face turns **red** when she feels shy.

Sometimes

by

Keith Baker

Sometimes I am happy.

ometimes I am cold.

I like who I am.

I like what I do.

Sometimes I am up.

Sometimes I am down.

I like who I am.

I like what I do.

Sometimes I am red.

Sometimes I am blue.

I'm all of these things.
What about you?

Think Critically

1 What kinds of feelings does the alligator have?

2 What does the alligator mean when he says he is "blue"?

3 What kinds of things does the alligator like to do?

4 What things do you like about yourself?

Vocabulary POWER

Family Day ▼

VOCABULARY

family

picnics

uncle

cousin

share

This is my **family**. Here are my sister, my mother, my father, and me.

My father's brother is my **uncle**.

My uncle has a son named Jake. Jake is my **cousin**.

We eat outside for **picnics**.

My brother, my sister, and I **share** a drink.

Family Day

Family picnics are a thrill!
Uncle Peter starts the grill.

Mom gets hot dogs, corn, and meat.
Dad cuts carrots for a treat.

Aunt Kim and Grandpa Lee
pour us lemonade and tea.

Cousin Beth and her friend Helen share a piece of watermelon.

I sit and watch with baby Kay,
and enjoy our happy family day!

Related Vocabulary

Picnic Food

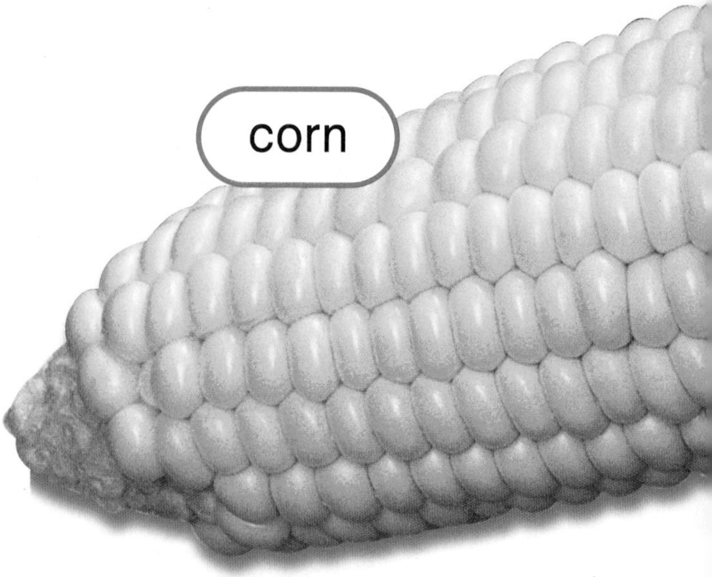
corn

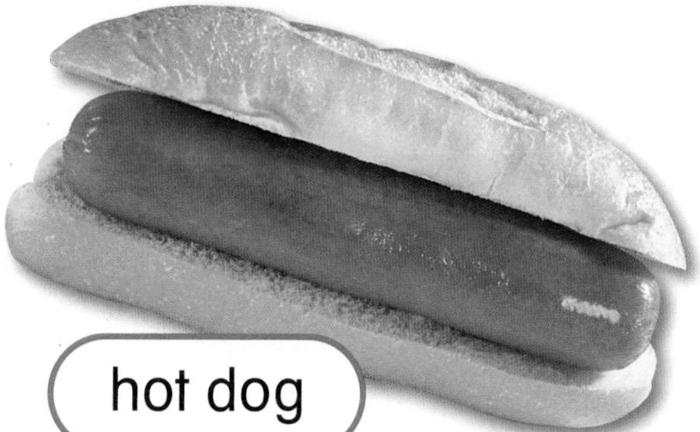
hot dog

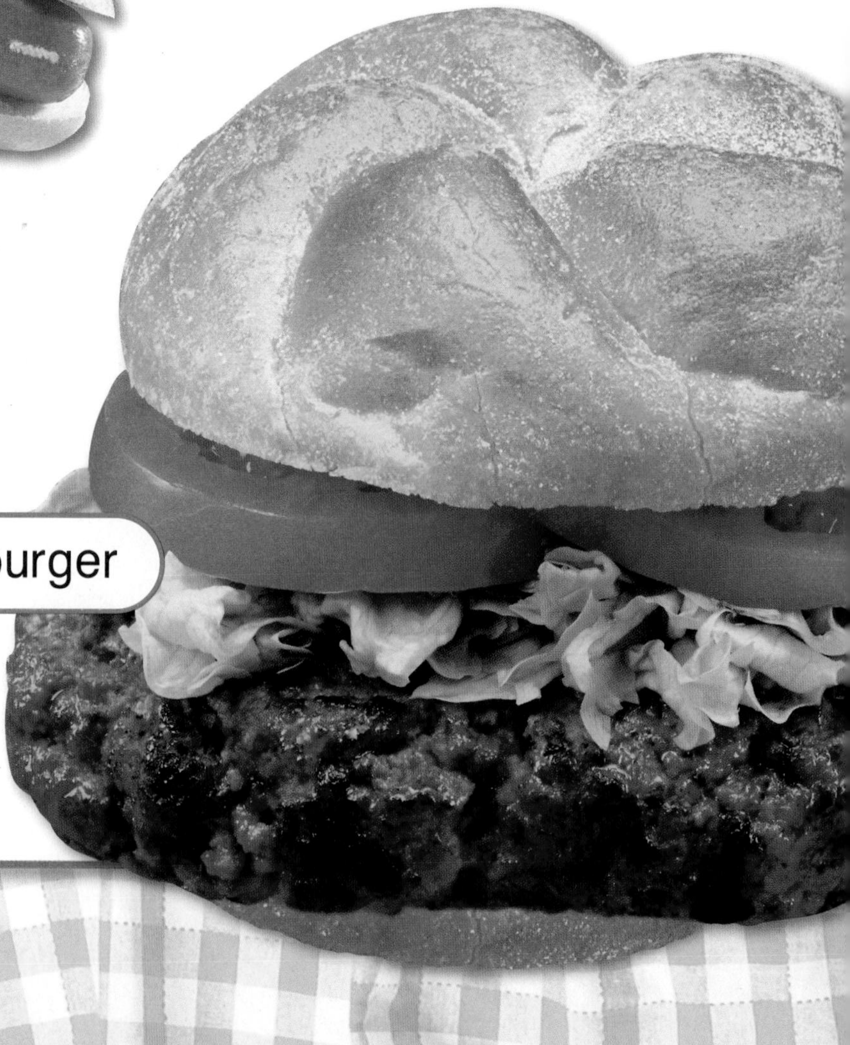
hamburger

pie

Think Critically

1. What does the family do to get ready for the picnic?

2. What foods do you think the family eats first and last?

3. What would you like to eat at a picnic? Why?

4. What do you like to do with your family?

47

Vocabulary POWER

Best of Friends ▼

VOCABULARY

pictures

friend

party

ride

bikes

paint

Debbie and I play together. She is my **friend**.

We play with face **paint**.

My friends came to my birthday **party**.

I am looking at family **pictures**.

We **ride** our **bikes** after school.

Best of
Friends

by Loreen Leedy

Uncle Bill came over one day.
"What are you doing?" he asked.

"I'm looking at my scrapbook," I said.
"It has pictures of all my friends."

"Who is your best friend?" asked Uncle Bill.

"Well . . . ," I said. "I'll show you."

"Who is this boy looking at ladybugs?" asked Uncle Bill.

"That's Jeff," I said. "He loves bugs."

"Who is the girl with the balloons?" asked Uncle Bill.

"That's Liz," I said. "I went to her party."

"Maybe Liz is my best friend."

"Who is this muddy boy?" asked
Uncle Bill.

"That's Nick," I said. "We always ride
bikes together."

"Maybe Nick is my best friend."

"Who is this girl with purple paint on her face?" asked Uncle Bill.

"That's Maria," I said. "She loves to paint, just like me."

"So, who is your best friend?" asked Uncle Bill.

"I have lots of friends," I said. "But maybe my very best friend is . . .

. . . my dog, Buzz!"

WOOF!

Think Critically

1. What does the boy like to do with his friends?

2. What clues tell you that Buzz is the boy's very best friend?

3. What do you like to do with your friends?

4. What things do you like to do that the boy also likes to do?

Vocabulary POWER

Our Needs ▼

VOCABULARY

food

grow

clean

weather

safe

breathe

I eat healthful **food** for lunch.

This helps me **breathe** under water.

We wash our dog to keep her **clean**.

Sunny **weather** helps flowers bloom.

I **grow** taller each year.

Police officers help keep us **safe**.

Our Needs

You need food to live.
Healthful foods give you energy.
They also help you grow.

food

You need water to live. Drinking clean water helps you stay healthy. Washing with water helps you stay clean.

water

You need a home to live in.
Your home keeps you warm or cool.
It keeps you dry in wet weather.
Your home also keeps you safe.

mobile home

apartment

cabin

69

You need air to live. You breathe air when you are awake. You breathe air when you are asleep. Clean air helps you think, run, and play.

family

You need a family and friends. Your family and friends make you feel special. You care about them, and they care about you.

Think Critically

1. What do you need to live?

2. Where do you get the things you need to live?

3. What other things do you need?

4. How does your home keep you safe?

71

LESSON 5

Unit Review

Review Vocabulary with a Play

STORIES ON STAGE

The Lion and the Mouse

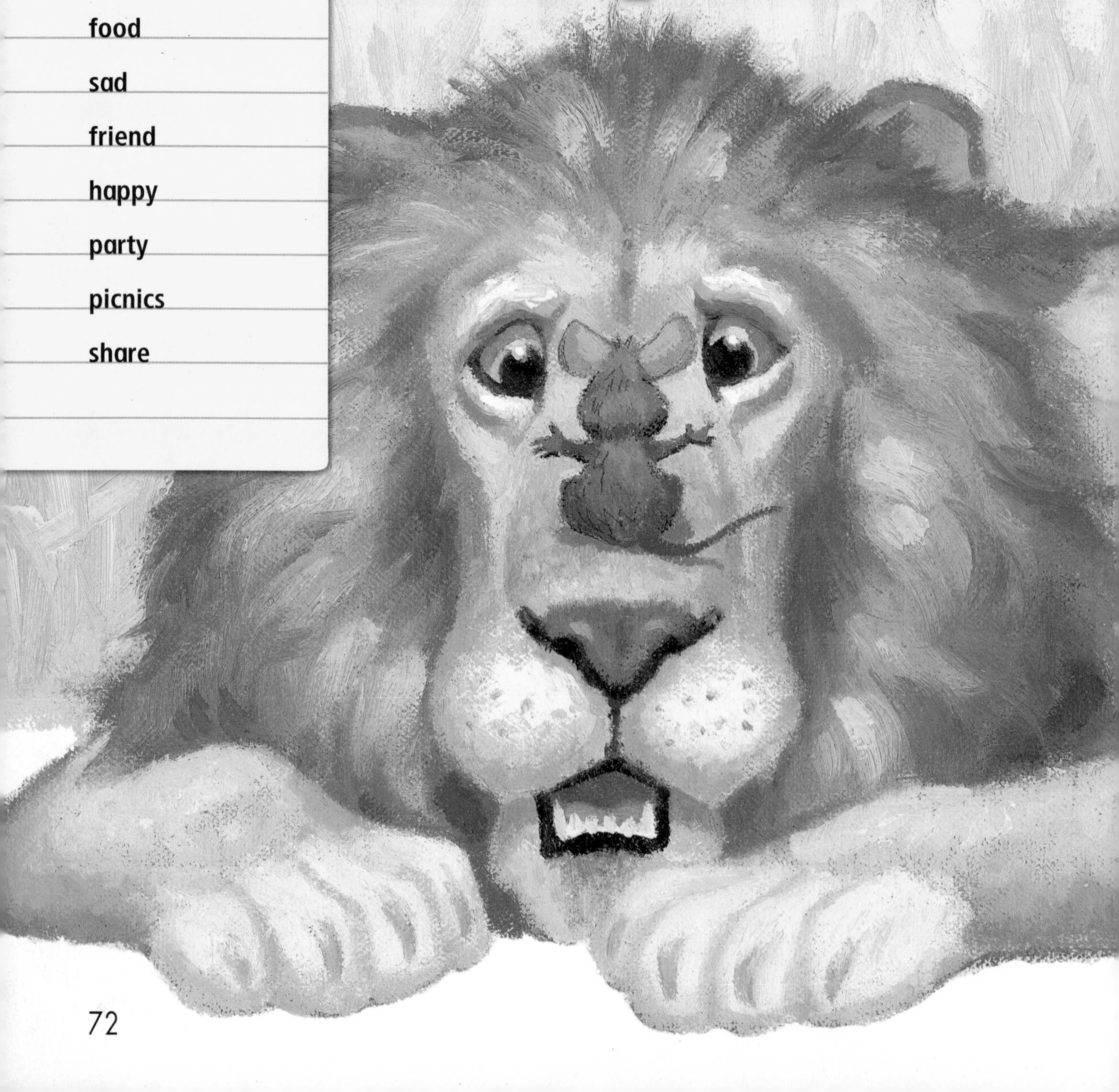

Review

VOCABULARY

- food
- sad
- friend
- happy
- party
- picnics
- share

Characters

Narrator

Lion

Mouse

Monkeys

73

Narrator: Once upon a time, a big lion saw
a little mouse walking by.

Lion: Stop, little mouse! I'm hungry.
You look good to eat.

Mouse: A mouse is not good food for a lion. Please let me go. One day I will help you if you do.

Lion: You may go, little mouse.

Monkeys: How can a little mouse help a big lion?

Narrator: Later that day the little mouse
saw the big lion in a net.

Lion: Help! Help!

Mouse: Don't be sad, Lion. I can help you.
I will cut the net with my teeth.

Monkeys: Can a little mouse cut a big net?

Narrator: The little mouse cut the net! The lion was set free.

Lion: You did it, Mouse! You are a good friend.

Mouse: I am happy that I could help you, Lion.

Lion: Let's have a big party.

Mouse: Yes, we can have a picnic. Picnics are fun! Then we can share good food with our friends.

Monkeys: A little animal can be a big help!

Review Activities

Think and Respond

1. What makes you happy? How do you show it?

2. How do the family members in "Family Day" help one another?

3. What things do the friends do together in "Best of Friends"?

4. What helps you live and grow?

5. What did you learn from reading "Family Day" and "Best of Friends"?

Match It

Use two sets of Word Cards.

1. Put the cards face down. Pick up two.
2. Are the words the same?
   If not, put them down again.
   If they are, say a sentence with the word.
   Then keep the cards.
3. Take turns. The person with the most cards wins!

bikes

cousin

happy

LANGUAGE STRUCTURE REVIEW

Describing Words

List three of your favorite things. Then think of a describing word that tells about each thing. Write each describing word in front of the thing it describes. Read your list to a friend.

cute	puppy
big	kite
white	snow

SING ALONG

Better Together

Sometimes we need to work together
To help each other, to build a team.
Sometimes we need to work together
To get the job done!

Sing to the tune of
"Here We Go 'Round the Mulberry Bush."

Setting

Every story has a setting.

√ The **setting** is **where** and **when** the story happens.

Read this story.

Cat Cools Off

One hot summer day, Cat and Duck played by the big pond. Duck jumped in the water to get cool.

Cat didn't like the water. She went under the big tree. It was cool there, too.

To understand the setting, ask yourself

■ **Where** does the story happen?

■ **When** does the story happen?

Setting	
Where	by the big pond
When	one hot summer day

Try This

▶ Read this story.

Reading Together

One morning at school, Anna was reading a book about the sun. Miguel came over. He wanted to read about the sun, too.

"I have a good idea," said Anna. "We can read together."

Miguel sat next to Anna and started to read. Reading together was fun!

Copy this chart. Complete it to show the setting.

Setting	
Where	
When	

Vocabulary POWER

On the Ranch ▼

VOCABULARY

feed

treat

strong

healthy

afternoon

fence

broken

barn

The cows gather near the red **barn**.

This man can lift a lot.
He is **strong**.

I **feed** the rabbit a carrot.

The horse eats beside the **fence**.
Part of the fence is **broken**.

They walk home from school
in the **afternoon**.

The boy eats a **treat**.
The milk will help him
stay **healthy**.

ON THE RANCH

My name is Ed. I live on a ranch
with my family. We take care of
many animals. Everyone has to help
with the work. I do some jobs when
I am not in school.

In the morning I help my sister feed the horses. The horses eat lots of hay. Carla and I give them oats as a special treat. Good food keeps the horses strong and healthy.

In the afternoon I help my brother check the fence around the ranch. The fence keeps our cows in so they don't get lost. If the fence is broken, Miguel and I have to fix it.

In the evening my father and I bring the horses back to the barn. We brush and clean them. Then we put them in their stalls.

The horses are tired from their day of work. So am I!

Think Critically

❶ How does Ed help on the ranch?

❷ What other jobs might there be on a ranch?

❸ How is Ed's family like the family in "Family Day"?

❹ What jobs do you do at home?

95

Vocabulary POWER

Build Together ▼

VOCABULARY

together

building

carry

teams

proud

finished

beautiful

We work **together**.

Teams of children play soccer together.

He can **carry** the wood.

They feel **proud** of the good job they did.

This house is not **finished** yet.

People work in this **building**. They are proud of how **beautiful** it looks.

BUILD TOGETHER

People must work together to make a building. First, they look at drawings of the building. These drawings help them know how to make the building.

These workers are ready to build. They will use rollers to make the land flat.

workers

roller

bulldozer

Workers use bulldozers to push rocks and mud and dump trucks to carry dirt. They use concrete mixers to hold wet concrete. Concrete keeps the building together.

crane

dump truck

excavator

Some teams of workers put the pieces together. Other teams pour the concrete.

team

concrete mixer

concrete

The workers can be proud when they are finished. They know that they worked together to make a beautiful building!

front-end loader

crane

dump truck

roller

Think Critically

1 What do the workers do before they build?

2 How do teams of workers build a building?

3 Why do the workers use machines?

4 When do you work with other people?

Vocabulary POWER

On the
Job with
Dr. Martha
Smith ▼

VOCABULARY

vet

sometimes

medicine

playful

examine

someone

A **vet** is an animal doctor.

I kick the ball to my **playful** puppy.

Someone is taking the dogs for a walk.

Sometimes my cat plays. Sometimes he just sits with me.

Let's **examine** the leaf.

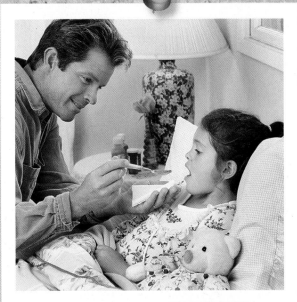

My dad gives me **medicine** when I am sick.

On the Job with Dr. Martha Smith

by Claire Daniel
photographs by Rick Friedman

rabbit

My name is Dr. Smith. I am a vet at an animal shelter. A shelter is a place where animals are taken when they need a home. My job is to keep the animals healthy.

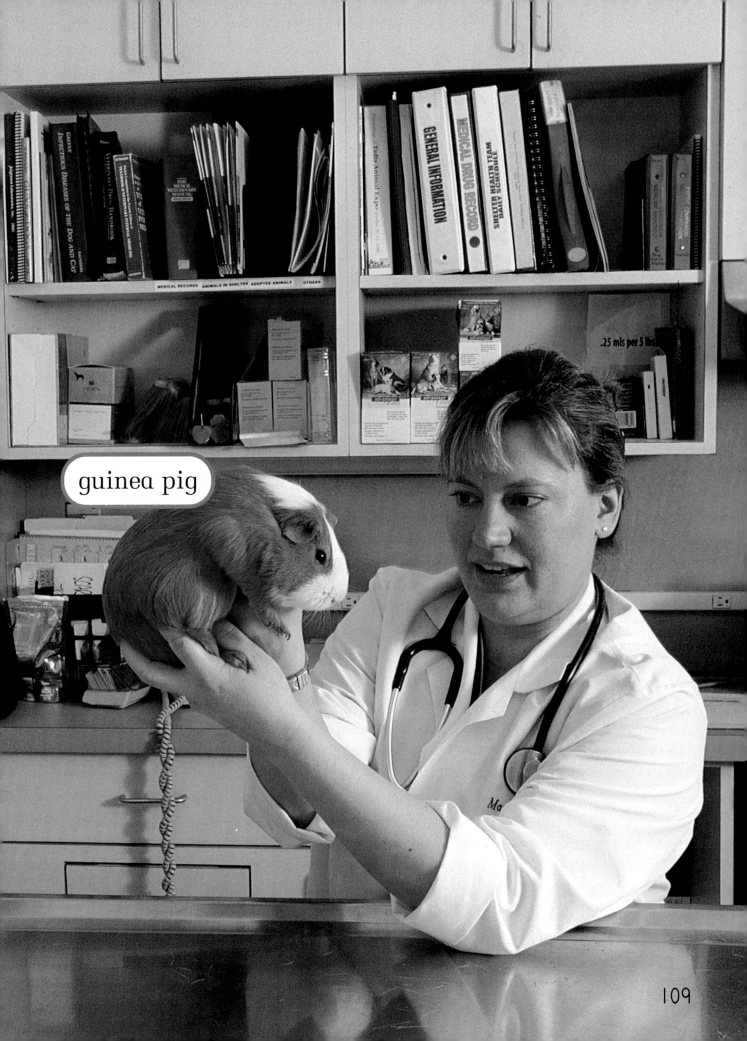

guinea pig

109

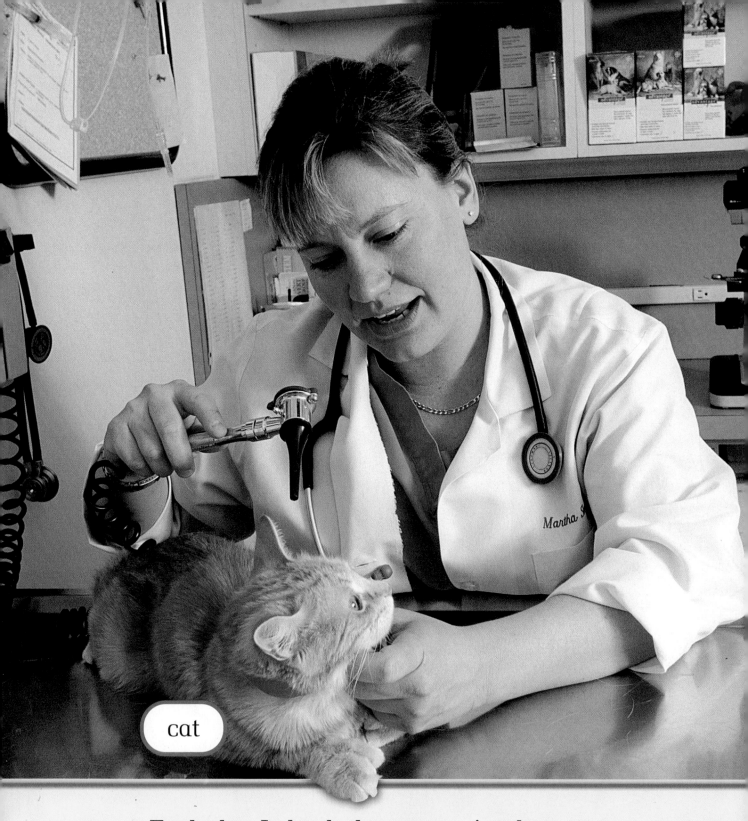

cat

Each day I check the new animals to
see if any of them are sick. Sometimes
I have to give them shots to make
them feel better.

This is a new cat named Muffin. A man
found her and brought her to the shelter.
She needed medicine when she got here.
Now she is very playful.

dogs

This worker is leading two new dogs into the shelter. She will give them a bath. Then I will examine them.

I check the dogs' eyes and teeth after
they take a bath. I make sure that their
eyes and teeth are clean and healthy.

Both dogs are healthy. They look happy
to be here at the shelter.

I think they would be happier
if they belonged to someone.

I love being a vet at the shelter because I help sick animals become healthy. When they are healthy, they can go home with someone. This family has found a cat to take home.

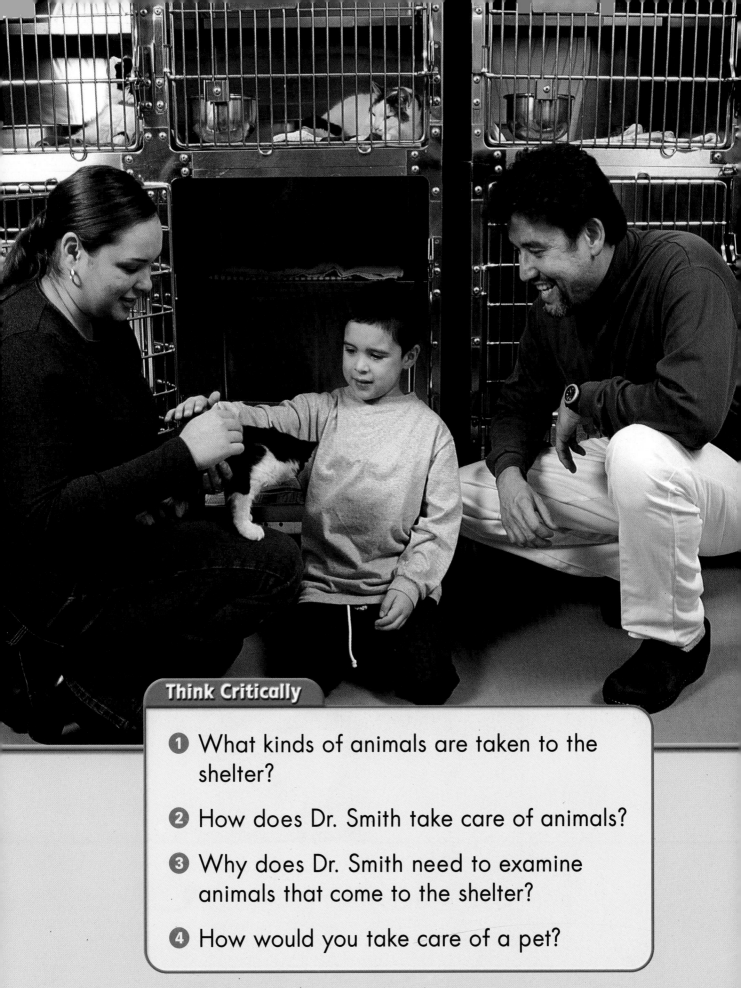

Think Critically

1 What kinds of animals are taken to the shelter?

2 How does Dr. Smith take care of animals?

3 Why does Dr. Smith need to examine animals that come to the shelter?

4 How would you take care of a pet?

117

Vocabulary POWER

Little Lumpty ▼

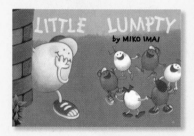

VOCABULARY

always

remember

ladder

mistake

tremble

blanket

Go up the **ladder**.

It was a **mistake** to carry so many books.

I **remember** reading many books when I was little.

I **tremble** when I am scared. That means I shake a little bit.

The **blanket** keeps the baby warm.

The sun **always** sets at the end of the day.

LITTLE

LUMPTY

by MIKO IMAI

In the little town of Dumpty there was a high wall.
Humpty Dumpty had fallen from it long, long ago.
But people still remembered him.

Every day children played by the wall and sang,
"Humpty Dumpty sat on the wall.
Humpty Dumpty had a great fall."

Little Lumpty loved the wall and always
dreamed about climbing to the top.
"Don't ever do that," Lumpty's mother said.
"Remember, all the king's horses and all the king's
men couldn't put Humpty Dumpty together again."

But Lumpty couldn't stop
thinking about the wall.
One day on his way home
from school, he found
a long ladder and dragged
it over there.

He climbed up . . .
and up . . . and up.

At last he reached the top. "Oh, there's my house!
And there's my school! I can almost touch the clouds!"

Lumpty was so happy that he danced along
like a tightrope walker.
"If only my friends could see me now!"

But then Lumpty looked down. **It was a big**

mistake! His legs began to shake and tremble.

"Oh, no! I don't think I can get back to the ladder.
What if I'm not home by dinnertime?"
It was getting dark and the birds were flying home
to their nests, but still Lumpty could not move.
Suddenly he remembered Humpty Dumpty's great fall.

"Help! Help!" Lumpty screamed.

Everyone in town rushed outside to see what was wrong.

"How can we save him?" asked an old man.
"We need a big blanket!" said Lumpty's mother,
and she ran home to get one.

They stretched it out at the bottom of the wall.

"Jump, Lumpty, jump!

Jump, Lumpty, jump!"

Lumpty took a deep breath and
threw himself into the dark night air.

He bounced once,

twice,

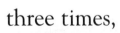

three times,

and then came safely to rest on the blanket.

"Mommy, I'm sorry. I just had to see what it would be like on top."

He was so glad to be home.

"But I still love that wall," he whispered to the moon just before he fell asleep.

Think Critically

1. Why does Lumpty's mother tell him not to climb the wall?

2. Why does Lumpty climb the wall?

3. How does the town help Lumpty?

4. How would you have helped Lumpty?

LESSON 10

Unit Review

Review Vocabulary with a Play

STORIES ON STAGE

The Little Red Hen

Review

VOCABULARY

barn

someone

carry

blanket

feed

afternoon

medicine

vet

finished

together

treat

remember

always

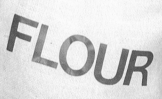

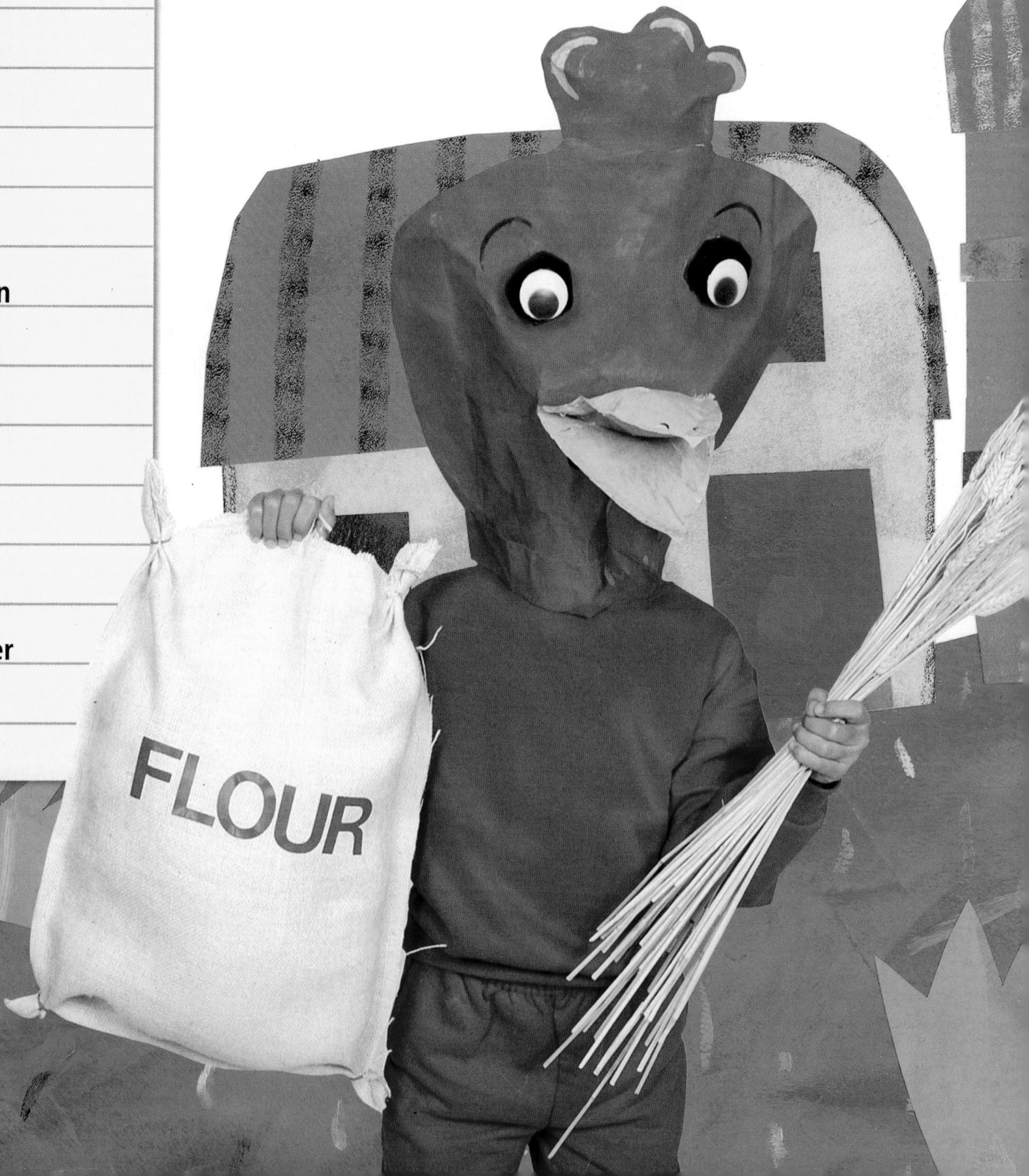

Little Red Hen

Cat

Dog

Duck

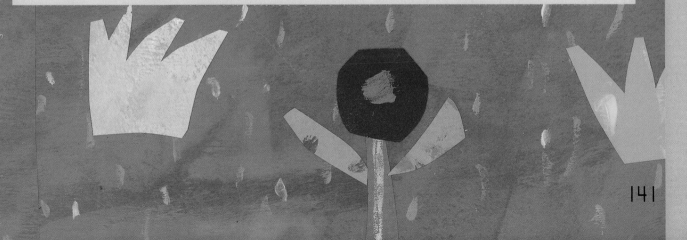

 I found these seeds in the barn. I want to plant them. Will someone help me?

 I want to take a nap.

 I want to play in the yard.

 I want to swim in the lake.

 Then I will plant the seeds myself.

 Now I need to carry the wheat home.
Will someone help me?

 I need to clean my feathers.

 I need to bark at the neighbors.

 I need to drink my milk.

 Then I will carry it myself.

 Now I have to grind the wheat into flour.
Will someone help me?

 I have to find my blanket.

 I have to feed my ducklings.

 I have to chew on my toys.

 Then I will grind it myself.

 Now I need to make the flour into bread.
Will someone help me?

 I need to go to the store this afternoon.

 I need to get medicine from the vet.

 I need to tease the dog.

 Then I will make the bread myself.

145

 The bread is finished. It smells so good!

 I can help you eat it.

 We can eat the bread together.

 It can be a treat for all of us.

 Oh, no. I remember that you did not help me.

 We're very sorry.

 We should always help our friends.

 We will always help you from now on.

 Then you may help me eat the bread. Who will help me clean up?

 We will!

Review Activities

Think and Respond

1. How does Ed help on the ranch?

2. What machines help workers make buildings?

3. How are Dr. Martha Smith and Ed alike?

4. Why does Little Lumpty need help?

5. Why do the Little Red Hen's friends help her clean up at the end of the play?

VOCABULARY REVIEW

Word Chairs

1. Set your chairs in a circle. Tape a word card onto each chair.

2. Walk around the circle until your teacher says "Stop!" Then sit in the chair nearest you.

3. Be ready to use your word in a sentence when it is your turn!

examine

LANGUAGE STRUCTURE REVIEW

Ask and Answer Questions

Find out what your partner thinks about the selections in this unit. Ask and answer these questions.

Who is your favorite character?

Which is your favorite selection?

What is the setting?

Why do you like this selection best?

SING ALONG

Growing and Changing

Things are growing, things are changing,

All the time, all the time.

Growing in so many ways,

Changing almost every day,

Watch them grow, watch them change!

Sing to the tune of "Frère Jacques."

Cause and Effect

√ A **cause** makes something happen.

√ An **effect** is what happens.

Read these sentences.

The wind blew hard. Rudy's hat blew away.

To find an effect, ask yourself
What happened?

To find the cause of the effect, ask yourself
Why did it happen?

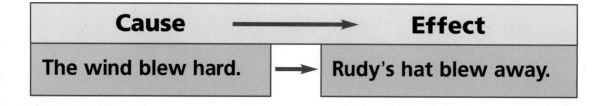

Cause	→	Effect
The wind blew hard.	→	Rudy's hat blew away.

Try This

▶ Read these sentences.

The sunflower got a lot of water and sunlight. It grew to be 5 feet tall!

Copy this chart. Write the cause and the effect.

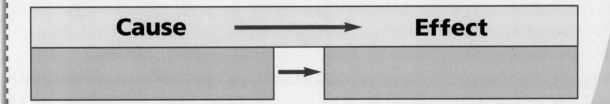

Cause	⟶	Effect
	→	

Changing El Paso ▼

VOCABULARY

glad

railroad

dam

factories

highways

products

The **railroad** goes from city to city.

A **dam** holds back the water.

I feel **glad** when I can go to the park.

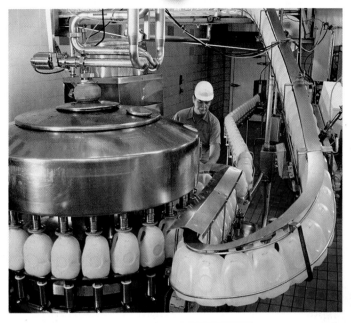

This factory makes **products**, such as orange juice.

My father works in one of the **factories** in his town.

Trucks travel on **highways** across the United States.

Changing El Paso

In 1848 the town of El Paso, Texas, became a part of the United States. Before that it belonged to Mexico. A long road ran through El Paso. People traveling by horse and wagon were glad to stop there.

In 1881 a railroad came to El Paso. The railroad helped people get to the town. It also helped people get the things they needed. Many people moved to El Paso because of the railroad. The town grew into a small city.

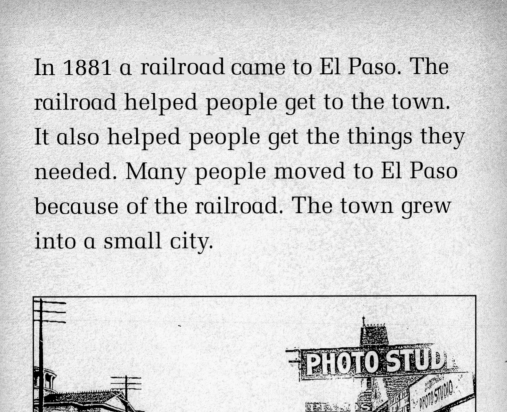

train

dam

In 1916 a dam was built near El Paso. The dam helped people get water for their farms and ranches. This helped people grow food and raise animals. Many more people came to El Paso. The small city grew fast.

El Paso today

Today El Paso is a large city with many factories. Big roads and highways pass through the city. Trucks, planes, and trains take El Paso's people and products to all parts of the United States.

In a City

highway

airport

factory

bridge

skyscraper

road

Think Critically

❶ How did El Paso change over the years?

❷ How did the railroad, dam, and highway make life easier in El Paso?

❸ What other things change in a city?

❹ How do you think your city has changed?

Vocabulary POWER

Storms ▼

VOCABULARY

dangerous

thunder

lightning

spin

predict

computers

prepare

Lightning looks bright and pretty when it lights up the sky.

I cover my ears when I hear **thunder**.

This looks like a **dangerous** trick.

This person will **predict** the weather by using **computers** to find out about a storm.

My toy can **spin** fast.

You can do things to **prepare** for a storm.

Storms

Every day, people check the weather report. It tells them if it is going to be rainy or sunny, hot or cold. They may also learn that a big storm is coming. Storms can be dangerous.

thunderstorm

In a Thunderstorm
- Stay indoors.
- If you are outdoors, stay away from trees. Keep low to the ground.

Thunderstorms are storms that have rain, thunder, and lightning. Lightning is very dangerous. It can strike trees and telephone poles. It can also strike people.

hurricane

In a Hurricane
- Bring small objects inside.
- Cover windows.

Hurricanes are big storms that begin over the ocean. They have strong winds, high waves, and heavy rain. Hurricanes can cause floods. Their strong winds can blow down trees and buildings.

tornado

In a Tornado
- Go to the lowest floor of a strong building.
- If you are outdoors, lie down in a low place.

Tornadoes are storms with strong winds that spin very fast. Tornadoes can tear apart buildings. They can also pick up things and carry them away. Tornadoes have even picked up cars.

blizzard

In a Blizzard
- Stay indoors.
- If you are outdoors and cannot see, keep your hands on a fence or a wall. Follow it to a safe place.

Blizzards are winter storms. They have very heavy snow and strong winds. It is hard to see in a blizzard. It is also hard to walk because of the wind and the deep snow.

Scientists can predict when and where storms will arrive. They use computers and other tools to find out if it will be sunny or stormy.

Knowing that a storm is coming can help you prepare for it. Always follow the rules to stay safe.

Think Critically

1. What are some kinds of storms?

2. Why should people stay inside during a blizzard?

3. How can storms change the world around us?

4. What kinds of storms do you have where you live?

Weather Poems ▼

VOCABULARY

field

umbrellas

sea

during

shine

shower

heat

My grandfather drinks water to cool off from the **heat**.

I also cool down **during** an afternoon rain. A light rain **shower** feels good.

170

People can use **umbrellas** to keep off the sun or the rain.

The strong wind is moving the boat across the **sea**.

I can see the sun **shine** on the water.

The man and his dog walk through the grassy **field**.

WEATHER

POEMS

Rain

by Robert Louis Stevenson

The rain is raining all around,
It falls on field and tree,
It rains on the umbrellas here,
And on the ships at sea.

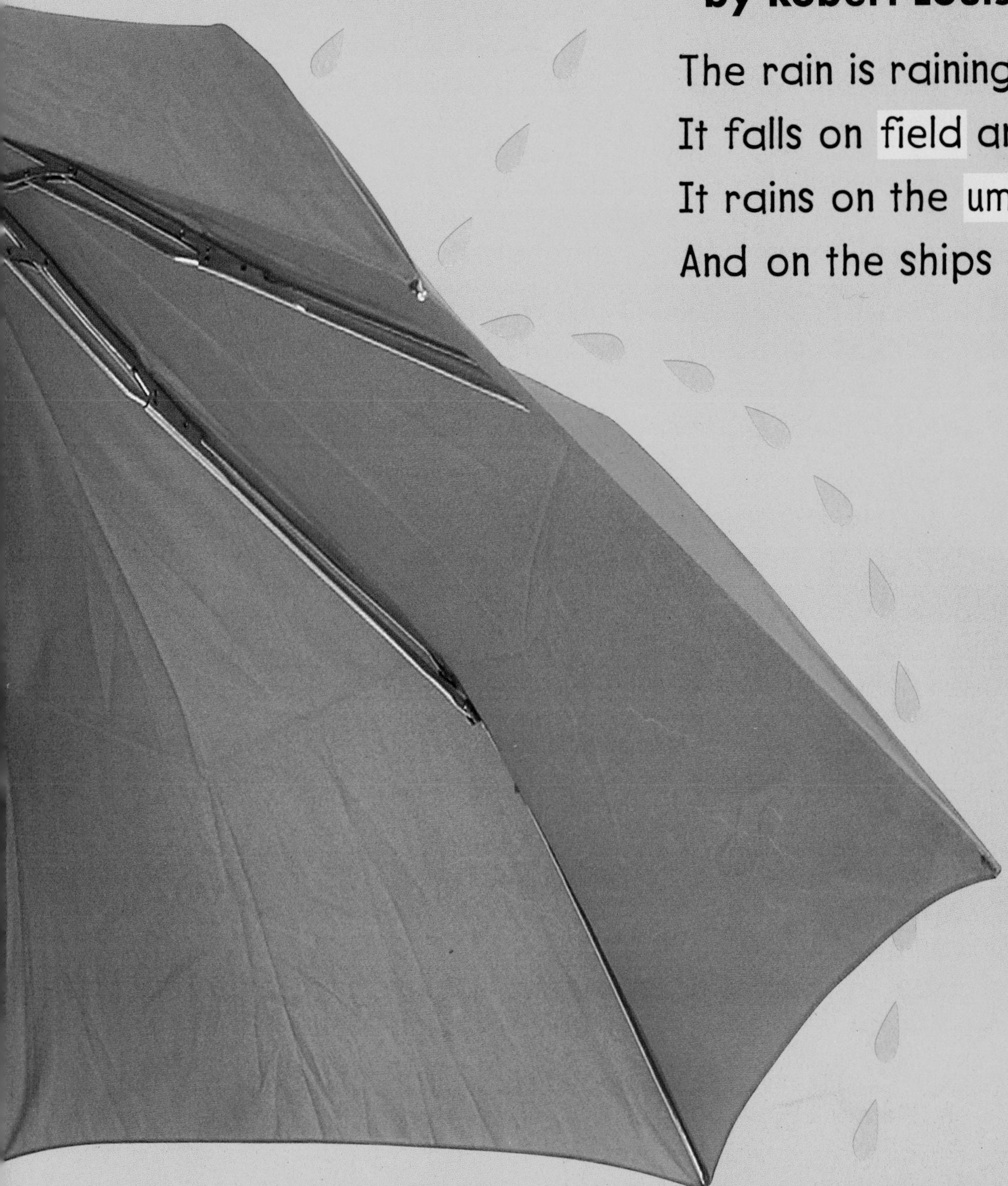

173

174

Daily Shower

by Francisco X. Alarcón

during
summer
it pours
every day

at five
on the dot
everybody
takes cover

but soon
it clears up
and the sun
comes back

streets
sidewalks
shine so neat
and clean

after
taking
their daily
shower

Change in the Weather

by Ilo Orleans

I think it would be very good
To have some snow and sleet
In summer when
We need it most
To drive away the heat.

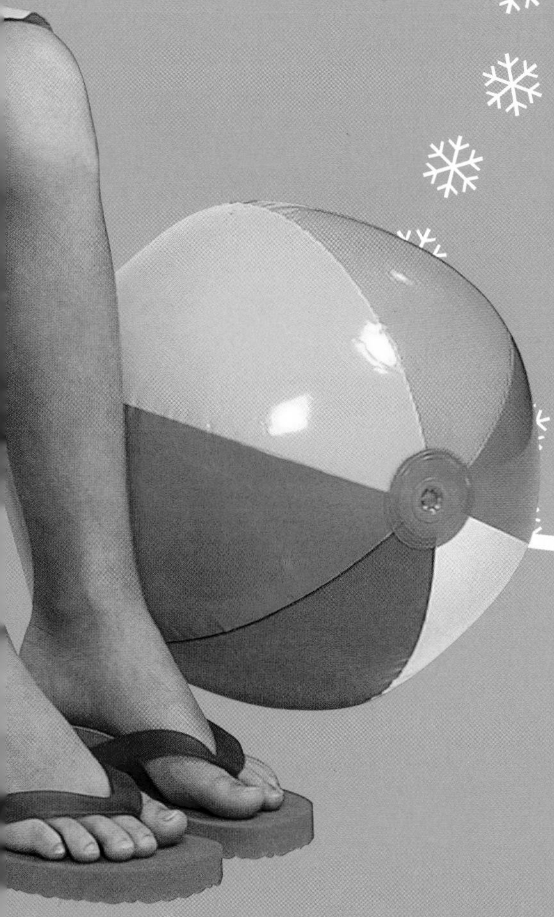

First Snow

by Marie Louise Allen

Snow makes whiteness where it falls.
The bushes look like popcorn-balls.
The places where I always play
Look like somewhere else today.

KINDS OF WEATHER

rainy

sunny

windy

180

snowy

stormy

Think Critically

1. What do the titles tell you about the poems?

2. How are the poems "Rain" and "Daily Shower" alike?

3. Why does the speaker in "Change in the Weather" want to have snow and sleet?

4. What kind of weather do you like best?

Vocabulary POWER

Fran's Flower ▼

VOCABULARY

flowerpot

soil

hungry

favorite

piece

juicy

surprise

A small plant is growing in the **soil**.

The lady plants flowers in a **flowerpot**.

182

I have a **surprise** for my dad.

The baby hugs her **favorite** toy.

My friends are **hungry**, so they eat lunch.

She is eating a **piece** of **juicy** watermelon.

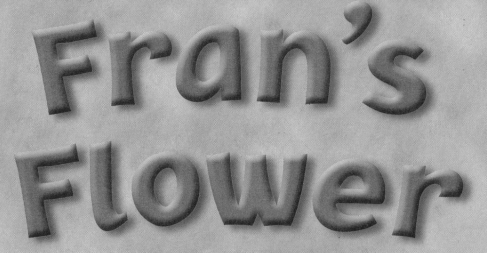

Fran's Flower

Written by Lisa Bruce

Illustrated by Rosalind Beardshaw

One day Fran found a flowerpot filled with soil. Poking out of the top was a tiny green tip. "I will grow this flower," Fran said to Fred.

She took it home.
"Grow flower," she said.
But the tip stayed tiny.

187

"I think this flower is hungry," Fran said.
So Fran went to the fridge.
Inside she found some of her favorite food.

She gave the flower a slice of pizza.

The next day Fran gave it a piece
of cheeseburger.

Then she gave it spaghetti, two chocolate chip cookies and a large spoonful of strawberry ice cream.

She even gave it one of Fred's juicy bones.

193

But the flower didn't grow. The tip
stayed tiny. Fran got fed up.
"Silly flower!" Fran said, and she
threw it out the back door.

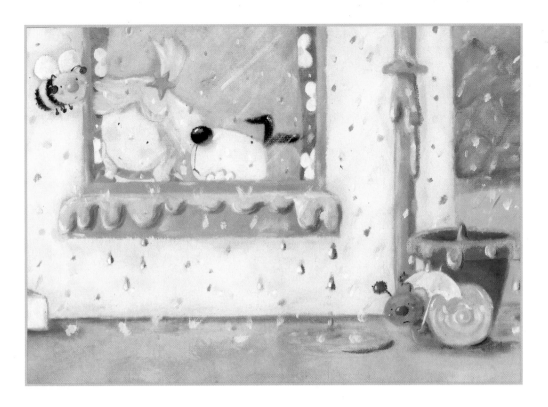

The flowerpot fell onto the ground
and rolled away. The rain fell on it.

The wind blew on it.

The sun shone on it.

197

Finally, the tiny green tip grew . . .

and grew . . .

and grew.

Until one day Fran and
Fred went outside to play.

198

When they opened the door,
a surprise was waiting . . .

A big beautiful flower–just for Fran!

Think Critically

1 Why does Fran get upset?

2 What causes Fran's flower to grow?

3 What do you think Fran learns about growing flowers?

4 What would you do if you found a flowerpot with a tiny plant?

Review Vocabulary with a Play

★ STORIES ON STAGE ★

The Apple Seed

Review

VOCABULARY

soil

field

spin

thunder

lightning

shower

surprise

shine

heat

glad

during

Characters

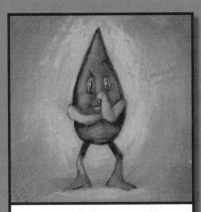

Apple Seed

Wind

Snow

Rain

Sun

Apple Seed: I can't find a place to grow. Snow, will you go away so I can find soil to grow in?

Snow: I don't want to go. I want to cover this field all year.

Apple Seed: Then I will ask the wind for help.

Apple Seed: Hello, Wind. Can you help me? Snow is covering the field. I can't find soil to grow in.

Wind: I will help you. I will blow and make the snow spin into the air.

Snow: You cannot blow me away. There is too much of me.

Wind: I cannot help you, Apple Seed. I am sorry.

Apple Seed: Then I will ask the rain for help.

Apple Seed: Hello, Rain. Can you help me? Snow is covering the field. I can't find soil to grow in.

Rain: I will help you. I will send thunder , lightning , and a rain shower to wash away the snow.

Snow: You cannot wash me away. It is too cold for rain today.

Rain: I cannot help you, Apple Seed. I am sorry.

Apple Seed: Then I will ask the sun for help.

Apple Seed: Hello, Sun. Can you help me? Snow is covering the field. I can't find soil to grow in.

Sun: I will help you. I have a surprise for snow! When I shine very brightly, my heat melts the snow.

Apple Seed: Thank you, Sun. I'm so glad I will have a place to grow.

Snow: Oh, no! The sun is melting me!

Apple Seed: Don't be sad, Snow. You can come visit me next year. I will be a tiny tree.

Snow: Thank you, Apple Seed. I will visit you every winter.

Apple Seed: Will you all come to visit me too?

Sun, Rain, Wind: We stay around all year. We'll watch you grow!

Apple Seed: I will be glad to have my friends with me during every season of the year.

Review Activities

Think and Respond

1. Think about your town. How do you think it is changing?

2. Think about the kinds of storms that happen where you live. What can you do to prepare for them?

3. Why do you think people write poems about weather?

4. What do you think Fran learns about growing flowers?

5. What do Apple Seed and Fran's flower need so they can grow?

Word Race

- Work with your group to make a sentence using a Vocabulary word. Write each word of your sentence on a card.

- Mix the words. Then trade cards with another group.

- Race the other group to put together each other's sentences!

LANGUAGE STRUCTURE REVIEW

Talk About Sequence

Work with three other children.

Take turns doing four different things, like standing up, walking, sitting down, and talking.

Then help each other tell what each of you did in the correct order.

Use words like **first, then, next,** and **finally**.

Be Creative!

Be creative
Every day—
Draw or write,
Find a way.
Dance or sing,
Put on a play—
Be creative!

 Sing to the tune of
"London Bridge Is Falling Down."

213

Main Idea

The **main idea** is the most important idea in a story or an article. It tells what the story or article is mostly about.

Read this article. What is the main idea?

People Who Create

People can create many things. Painters paint pictures. Potters shape clay. Authors write books. What do you like to create?

People can create many things is the main idea. It tells what this article is mostly about.

Try This

▶ Read this article.

Pets

Having a pet is a lot of work! All pets need to have good food and clean water. Sometimes they need to see the vet.

Dogs need to go for walks. Cats need exercise, too.

Birds, fish, and hamsters may seem easy to care for, but you still need to clean their homes.

Which sentence tells what this article is mostly about?

Having a pet is a lot of work!

Pets need to see the vet.

Dogs need to go for walks.

Cats need exercise.

You need to clean the homes of birds, fish, and hamsters.

Vocabulary POWER

Making a Picture Book ▼

VOCABULARY

illustrates

research

information

sketch

diagram

editor

bookstore

First, workers make a **sketch** of a house. Then they build it.

She **illustrates** her stories by drawing pictures.

i had a great geat time at camp!

An **editor** changes sentences to make them better.

I find **information** in books when I do **research**.

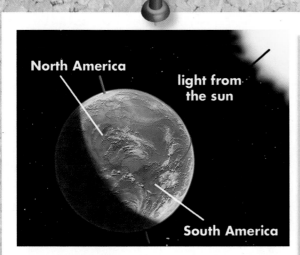

You can show things in a **diagram**.

North America

light from the sun

South America

Mom and I go to the **bookstore** to find a book I like.

Making a Picture Book

Loreen Leedy writes and illustrates picture books. Here are the steps she follows.

Research

First, she does research on things she wants to write about. She looks for information in books and on her computer.

Write and Sketch

Next, she uses her research to write the story. She makes sketches as she writes. A sketch is a quick drawing. She uses paint and artist's tools to complete the pictures.

Plan

Then she makes a book plan. This is a
diagram that shows what will be on each page.
After the book plan is made, she makes a
model of what the book will look like.

Publish

Her editor looks at the model and may ask for changes. The editor gives the pictures and the story to the publisher. The publisher makes them into the book you will find in the bookstore.

Computer Words

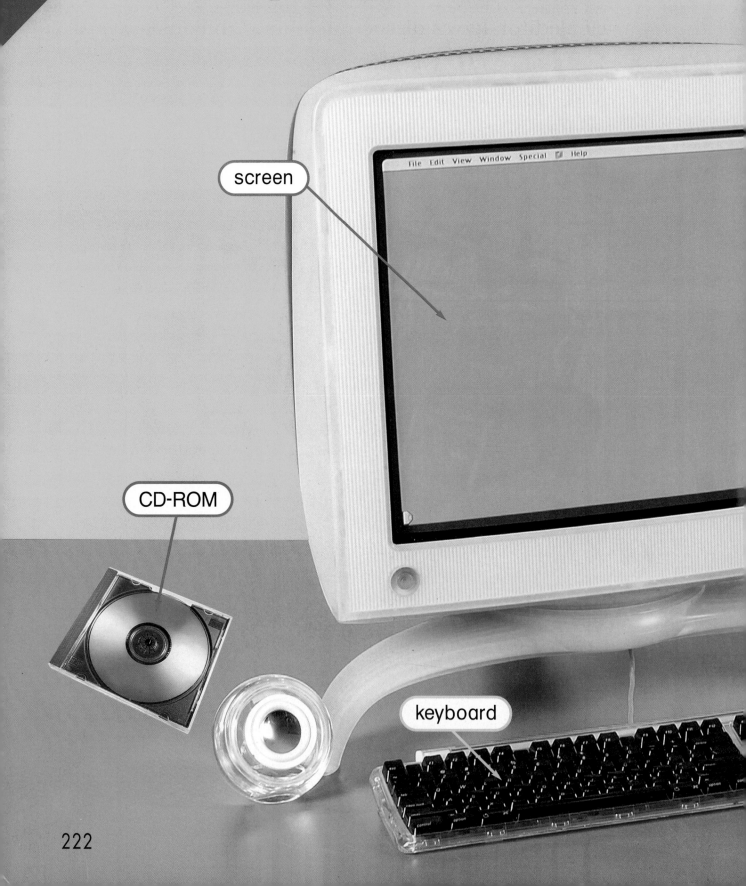

screen

CD-ROM

keyboard

File Edit View Window Special Help

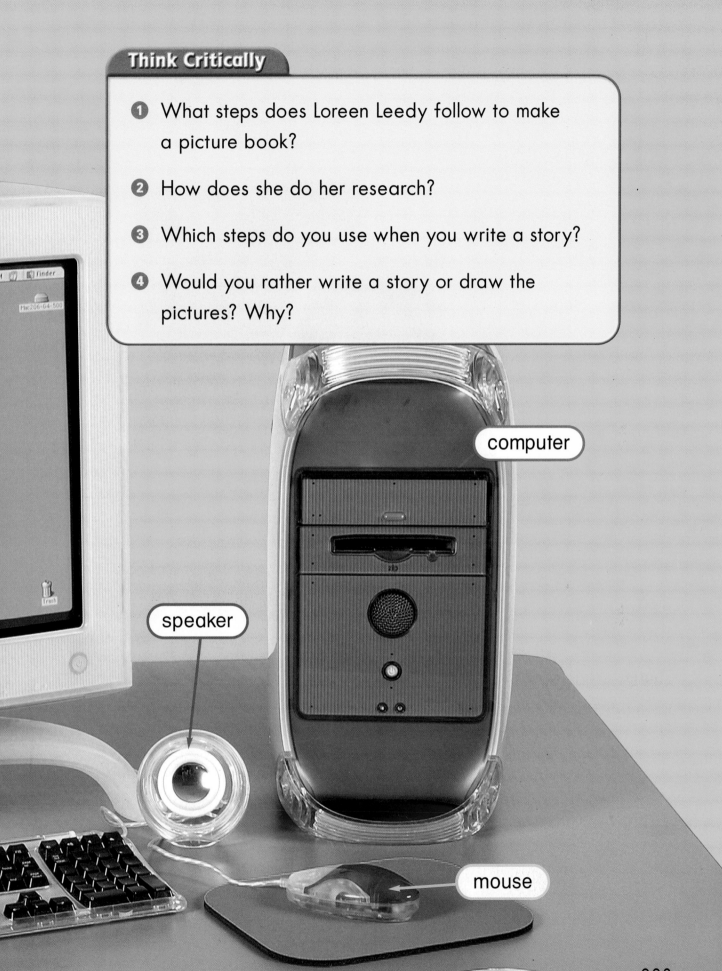

1. What steps does Loreen Leedy follow to make a picture book?

2. How does she do her research?

3. Which steps do you use when you write a story?

4. Would you rather write a story or draw the pictures? Why?

computer

speaker

mouse

Vocabulary POWER

Frog and Toad Are Friends ▼

VOCABULARY

quite

thought

porch

perhaps

stood

poured

terrible

asleep

I **poured** juice into a glass.

I don't know if I want to read or play.
Perhaps I will write on my **porch**.

The girl **stood** at the bus stop.

I **thought** about my homework.

It was not **quite** bedtime, but
I fell **asleep** fast.

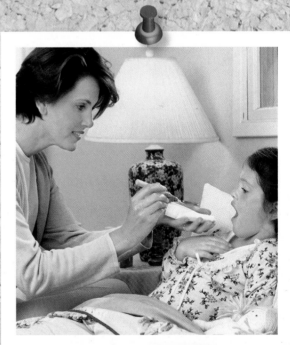

I am sick. I feel **terrible**.

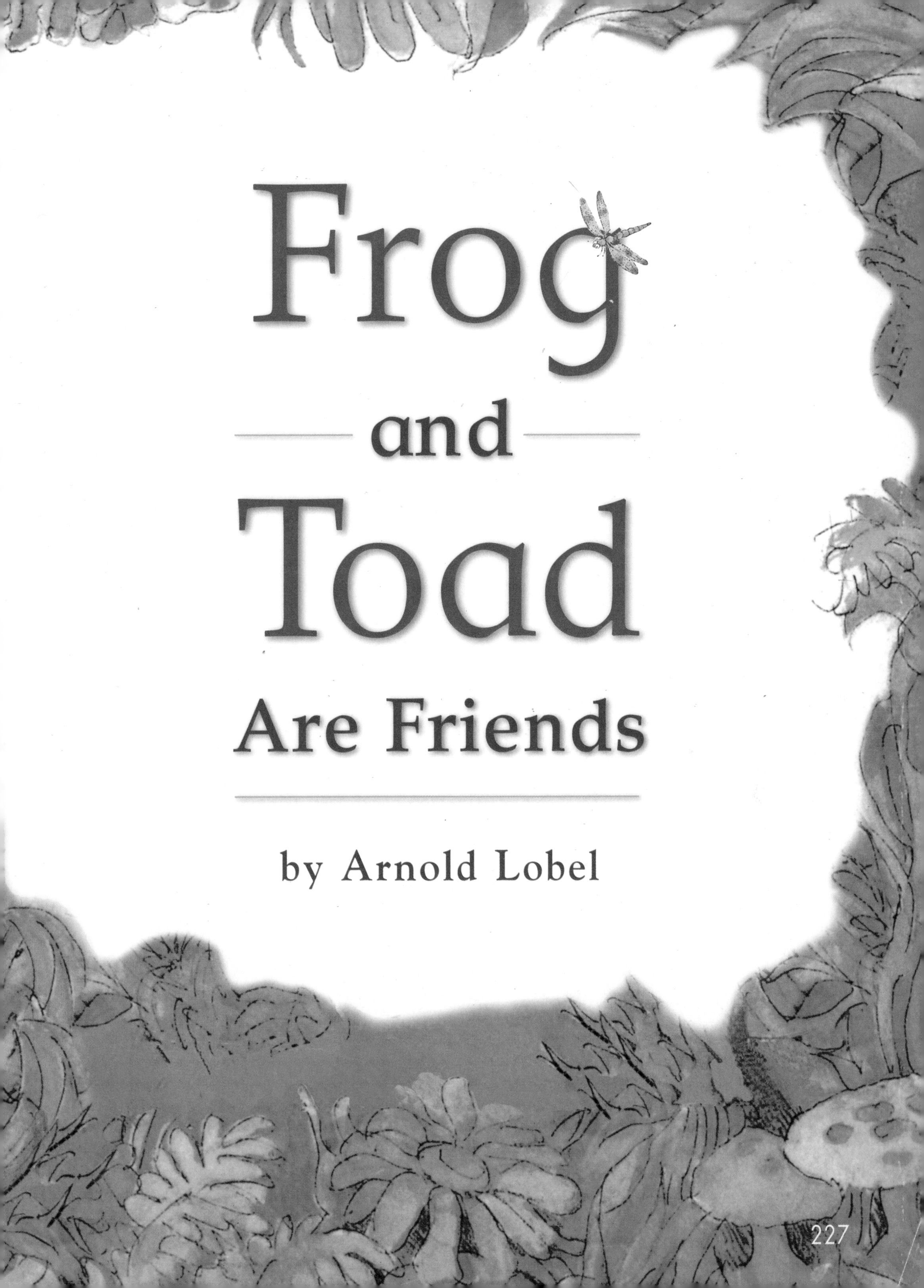

Frog
and
Toad
Are Friends

by Arnold Lobel

The Story

One day in summer

Frog was not feeling well.

Toad said, "Frog,

you are looking quite green."

"But I always look green,"

said Frog. "I am a frog."

"Today you look very green

even for a frog," said Toad.

"Get into my bed and rest."

Toad made Frog a cup of hot tea.

Frog drank the tea, and then he said,

"Tell me a story while I am resting."

"All right," said Toad.

"Let me think of a story to tell you."

Toad thought and thought.

But he could not think of a story

to tell Frog.

"I will go out on the front porch

and walk up and down," said Toad.

"Perhaps that will help me

to think of a story."

Toad walked up and down

on the porch for a long time.

But he could not think of a story

to tell Frog.

Then Toad went into the house

and stood on his head.

"Why are you standing

on your head?" asked Frog.

"I hope that if I stand on my head,

it will help me

to think of a story," said Toad.

Toad stood on his head

for a long time.

But he could not think

of a story to tell Frog.

Then Toad poured a glass of water
over his head.

"Why are you pouring water
over your head?" asked Frog.

"I hope that if I pour water
over my head,
it will help me to think
of a story," said Toad.

Toad poured many glasses of water
over his head.

But he could not think
of a story to tell Frog.

Then Toad began
to bang his head
against the wall.

"Why are you banging your head
against the wall?" asked Frog.
"I hope that if I bang my head
against the wall hard enough,
it will help me to think of a story,"
said Toad.

"I am feeling much better now, Toad,"
said Frog. "I do not think
I need a story anymore."

"Then you get out of bed
and let me get into it," said Toad,
"because now I feel terrible."

Frog said, "Would you like me
to tell you a story, Toad?"

"Yes," said Toad, "if you know one."

"Once upon a time," said Frog,

"there were two good friends,

a frog and a toad.

The frog was not feeling well.

He asked his friend the toad

to tell him a story.

The toad could not think of a story.

He walked up and down on the porch,

but he could not think of a story.

He stood on his head,

but he could not think of a story.

He poured water over his head,

but he could not think of a story.

He banged his head against the wall,

but he still could not think

of a story.

Then the toad did not feel so well,

and the frog was feeling better.

So the toad went to bed and

the frog got up

and told him a story.

The end.

How was that,

Toad?" said Frog.

But Toad did not answer.

He had fallen asleep.

Think Critically

1. Why does Frog ask Toad to tell him a story?

2. What things does Toad do to think of a story?

3. Why does Frog tell Toad a story?

4. How would you make a friend feel better?

Vocabulary POWER

Maria Martinez ▼

VOCABULARY

desert

pottery

scientists

ancient

decorated

husband

designs

famous

Scientists dig to find things from long ago.

Scientists dug this **pottery** out of the ground. It is very old, or **ancient**.

These pots are **decorated** with paint. An artist painted **designs** on them.

This **desert** is very hot in the daytime.

The **husband** and wife like to be together.

This is a statue of a **famous** President named Abraham Lincoln.

Maria Martinez

The Pueblo people of New Mexico have used the desert clay to make pottery for many years. Maria Martinez learned to make Pueblo pottery the way it was made in the past. She is an important part of Pueblo history.

Maria Martinez was born in the 1880s in New Mexico. As a young girl, Maria learned to make pottery from her aunt. Her aunt made pots the same way people in the pueblo had made them for years.

When Maria was older, scientists who study the way people lived a long time ago came to her pueblo. They found broken pieces of painted pottery.

The pottery was made by the ancient people who had lived in caves near Maria's pueblo. Maria wondered if she could make pottery like the pieces the scientists had found. She had never decorated her pottery before. Maria's husband was a good painter, and he agreed to paint designs on the pots she made.

Maria made many pots like these during her life. She also taught others to make pottery the way the ancient people made it. Maria's pottery became famous throughout the world. It showed people an important part of Pueblo life.

pottery

Think Critically

1 Why was Maria Martinez's pottery special?

2 How did she help keep the old Pueblo way alive?

3 What things have you learned from your family?

4 What things do you like to make?

Vocabulary POWER

All the Good Hands ▼

VOCABULARY

drifts

unload

stack

market

special

across

guides

cure

create

The smoke **drifts** through the air.

This boy likes to **create** art. He is making something **special** to show his favorite things.

246

The dog shows the man the way to go. It **guides** him **across** the room.

The workers **unload** the boxes and **stack** them.

You can buy many kinds of fresh food at the **market**.

The medicine will help the boy get better. It will help **cure** his illness.

All the Good Hands

by F. Isabel Campoy
illustrated by Yuyi Morales

The bread smells good!
The baker gets up early to make bread.
He uses his hands to shape the dough.
His helper pushes the dough into the oven
and bakes it golden brown.
The smell of hot bread drifts into windows
while most people are still asleep.

Fruits for sale!
The farmers bring fruits of many colors in big trucks from the country.
They use their hands to unload the boxes and stack the fruit they sell at the market.

251

Let's cross the street!
The woman uses her hands to hold on
to the guide dog. She follows her special
dog across the street. He guides her
safely to work.

There are many hands that help in my community from morning to night.
In every street and plaza, there are helping hands in my city.

254

I don't know what my hands will do when I get older. I don't know if they'll paint or cure animals. No matter what job I have, I will use my hands to help and to create.

Think Critically

❶ How do the farmers use their hands?

❷ How does the guide dog help the woman?

❸ Why do you think this selection is called "All the Good Hands"?

❹ How will you use your hands when you get older?

Review Vocabulary with a Play

STORIES ON STAGE

The Best Gift

Characters

Narrator

King

King's Helper

Old Man

Woman

Girl

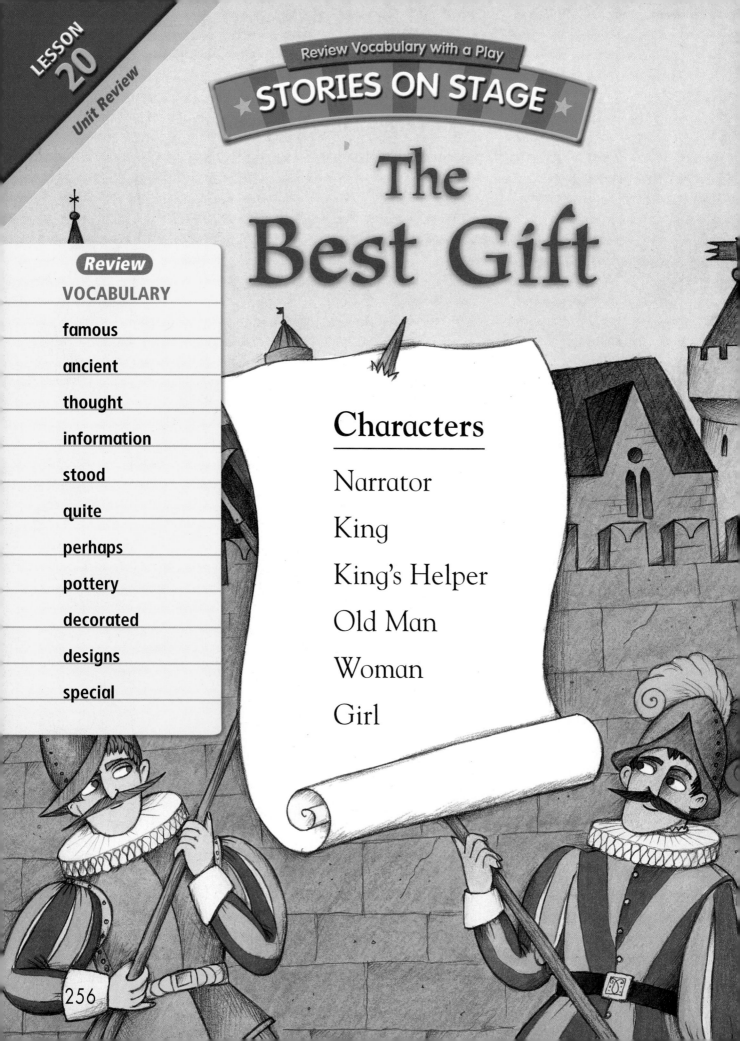

Narrator: A famous king lived in an ancient kingdom. The king had a problem. He didn't know how to choose someone to rule his kingdom after him.

King's Helper: I've thought of a way to solve your problem! You can have a contest. The person who brings the best gift will live in your castle and rule the kingdom one day.

King: I like that idea! Go and tell the people.

Narrator: The king's helper gave the people this information. All of them wanted to win the contest!

Narrator: Many people brought fine gifts. An old man came and stood in front of the king.

Old Man: I have brought you these beautiful jewels. I am sure they will be the best gift.

King: These jewels are quite beautiful.

King's Helper: Perhaps someone will bring you a better gift.

Narrator: Many more people brought fine gifts. A woman came and stood in front of the king.

Woman: I have brought you this beautiful pottery decorated with gold designs. I am sure it will be the best gift!

King: This pottery is quite beautiful.

King's Helper: Perhaps someone will bring you a better gift.

Narrator: Many more people brought gifts. The king could not choose the best one. Then a girl came and stood in front of him.

Girl: Dear King, I could not buy you a gift, so I drew a special picture. It is a picture of you.

Narrator: The king looked at the drawing for a long time.

King: This drawing is the best gift of all!

Girl: My family will be so happy!

Old Man: That drawing cannot be the best gift!

Woman: She didn't buy it—she made it herself!

King's Helper: Don't you see? That is why it is the best gift!

Narrator: From that day on, the girl and her family lived with the king. Someday his kingdom would belong to her.

261

Review Activities

Think and Respond

1. What steps does Loreen Leedy follow to make a picture book?

2. How does Toad try to think of a story to tell Frog?

3. How is Maria Martinez like the workers in "All the Good Hands"?

4. How do you use your hands to create?

5. Why does the king think the girl's picture is the best gift?

VOCABULARY REVIEW

Act It Out

1. Work with a group. Pick a Vocabulary word.

2. Act out a scene about the word.

3. Ask your classmates to guess the word.

4. The person who guesses correctly can choose the next word and act it out.

poured

Make Comparisons

Work with a small group. Take turns choosing an object in the room. Don't tell your group what you chose. Tell about the object by comparing it to other things. For example:

It is smaller than that book. It is bigger than this piece of chalk.

If no one guesses, let the group ask questions.

SING ALONG

Let's Celebrate

Let's celebrate our community.

Let's celebrate our history.

Neighborhood helpers and our family

Keep us safe and healthy.

Sing to the tune of
"Skip to My Lou."

Draw Conclusions

Sometimes you can use clues in a story to figure out things that an author does not tell you. This is called **drawing conclusions**.

Read this story.

A New Coat

Carey was getting ready for school. Her mother said, "Put on your new coat, Carey." Carey put on the coat. It kept her warm on the way to school.

To draw a conclusion, follow these steps:
1. Find the story clues.
2. Think about what you already know.
3. Use the clues and what you know to figure out what the author does not tell you.

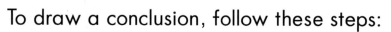

Story Clues	What You Know	Conclusion
Carey's coat kept her warm.	People wear coats when it is cold outside.	It was cold outside.

FOCUS SKILL

▶ Read this story. Use the story clues and what you already know to figure out what kind of pet Alex has.

The New Pet

Alex looked at his new pet, Spot. Spot looked very thirsty, so Alex gave him a bowl of water. Then he went to get Spot some food.

When Alex got back with the food, Spot wagged his tail and began to bark. Spot must have been hungry, too.

What kind of pet is Spot? Make a chart like this to show what helped you draw your conclusion.

Story Clues	What You Know	Conclusion

Vocabulary POWER

American Holidays ▼

VOCABULARY

celebrate

holidays

remember

history

country

flag

parades

important

We have fun on **holidays** like Cinco de Mayo.

We march in **parades** to **celebrate** Independence Day.

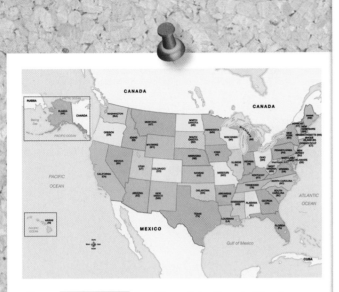

Our **country** is the United States of America.

This sculpture helps us **remember** four Presidents from long ago.

Every star on our **flag** is **important** because it stands for a state in our country.

The **history** of a country tells what happened long ago.

American Holidays

We celebrate special days in the United States. We call these days holidays. They help us remember our country's history. They also help us remember people who have made our country a great place.

 # Flag Day

June 14 is Flag Day. It is the day we celebrate our flag's birthday.

Many people in the United States fly the flag at home. Schools also fly the flag. Does your school have a flag? Cities and towns have parades and other celebrations to honor the flag.

Declaration of Independence

Independence Day

July 4 is Independence Day. It is the birthday of our country.

Many years ago on this day, the first American leaders decided the United States would be a free country. Each year on Independence Day, we celebrate and remember how our country began.

drum

Americans celebrate this day with games, concerts, parades, and speeches. Many people get together with friends and family for picnics.

Some cities also have huge fireworks shows. Thousands of people watch the shows each year.

Presidents' Day

In February we celebrate Presidents' Day. February was chosen because President George Washington and President Abraham Lincoln were born in that month. They were two of our country's important leaders.

Presidents' Day honors all the Presidents who have led our country.

Mount Rushmore

George Washington

Franklin D. Roosevelt

Thomas Jefferson

John F. Kennedy

Abraham Lincoln

275

American Places

The White House

Think Critically

1. What special holidays does America celebrate?

2. Why do people celebrate holidays?

3. What do you do to celebrate holidays?

4. What is your favorite holiday? Why?

Washington Monument

Lincoln Memorial

Statue of Liberty

Vocabulary POWER

Neighborhood Helpers ▼

VOCABULARY

neighborhood

police officers

mail carriers

post office

librarians

doctors

nurses

hospital

Your **neighborhood** is where you live. **Police officers** help keep it safe.

Workers sort the mail inside the **post office**.

Mail carriers bring letters to your home.

Librarians help people find books at the library.

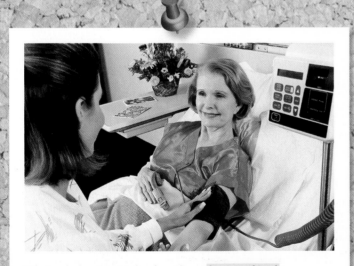

This woman is in the **hospital**. **Nurses** will care for her until she gets better.

Doctors help us when we are sick or hurt.

Neighborhood Helpers

People work in every neighborhood. They have jobs that help to make the neighborhood a good place to live.

Police Officers

You know that police officers help fight crime. Do you know how they move from place to place? Police officers ride in cars, on motorcycles, on bicycles, and on horses. They even fly in helicopters.

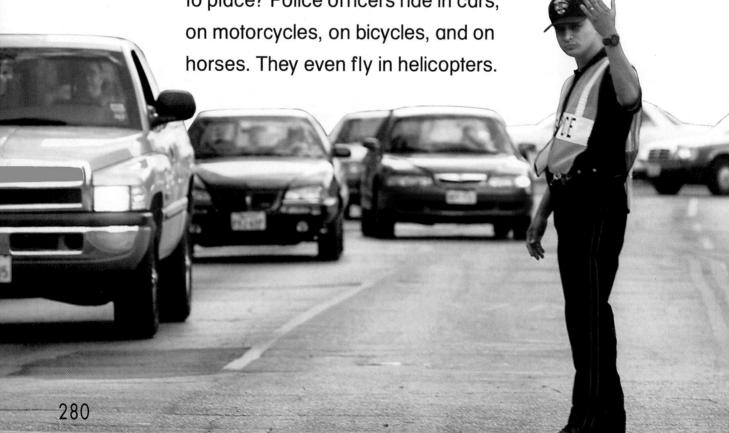

Mail Carriers

You know that mail carriers deliver letters and work at the post office. Do you know that mail carriers also watch over the neighborhoods where they deliver mail? If mail carriers see that someone is not picking up his or her mail, they call the police to check on that person.

Librarians

You know that librarians help you find and check out books. Do you know that they also help you answer questions? Librarians can help you find information from the Internet, magazines, CDs, and of course, books.

Doctors and Nurses

You know that doctors and nurses help people who are sick or hurt. Do you know that doctors go to school for many years to learn how the body works? Do you know that nurses care for people in many ways? They might take time to play with a sick child at the hospital or read a book to a person who cannot see.

Teachers

You know that teachers help you learn. Do you know the other things they do? Teachers plan each day's lesson very carefully. They think of new ways to teach information to their students. Teachers meet with parents and other school workers to decide how to help every child in their classroom. Some teachers also coach sports teams after school.

Neighborhood Helpers Web

teacher

librarian

mail carrier

nurse

police officer

Neighborhood Helpers

doctor

Think Critically

❶ What kinds of jobs are there in neighborhoods?

❷ What other ways do police officers help a neighborhood?

❸ Who are some other helpers in your neighborhood?

❹ What job would you like to have? Why?

Vocabulary POWER

Tree Story ▼

VOCABULARY

busy

bark

damp

discovered

crumbled

appeared

mound

sprouted

The bear is **busy** climbing up the tree. It holds onto the **bark** that covers the tree.

Rain made the soil **damp**. Then a seed **sprouted** out of the soil.

They **discovered** a bug on a log.

A rainbow **appeared** in the sky after a storm.

This is a big **mound** of dirt.

The old building **crumbled** into small pieces.

Tree Story

illustrated by
Alan and Lea Daniel

A maple tree grew tall in the forest.

Squirrels scampered in the tree's branches.

Blue jays flew in and out of the tree all day.

The tree was a busy place.

A family of barred owls looked out from a hollow high above.

A downy woodpecker pecked for insects that scurried beneath the tree's bark.

289

Carpenter ants built nests under the tree's bark.

Down it fell.

One day lightning struck the old tree.

Slugs moved in. Horned beetles and earwigs came.

A raccoon discovered a hole in the tree and built its den there.

Pill bugs and millipedes liked the cool, damp spaces between the old tree and the forest floor.

Some animals left, but new ones came.

In time, fungi, lichens, and moss covered the tree.

Toadstools and mushrooms appeared.

Earthworms tunneled and chewed. They helped turn the rotting tree into a mound of fine, black soil.

After many years, the old tree rotted and crumbled.

Then one day, in the very place the great, old tree once stood, a tiny, new tree sprouted.

And that was the beginning of a new tree story.

Think Critically

1. How does the tree change?

2. Why do different kinds of animals live in the tree at different times?

3. How is the tree like other communities you have read about?

4. What animals have you seen around trees?

Vocabulary POWER

The Emperor's Egg ▼

VOCABULARY

island

waddled

hatch

miserable

snuggle

slippery

throat

pouch

An **island** has water all around it.

Some baby animals **hatch** from eggs.

The ducks **waddled** when they walked. One duck has a white stripe around its **throat**.

The little kangaroo sits in its mother's **pouch**.

These animals do not feel **miserable** in cold weather. They **snuggle** together to keep warm.

They slide on the smooth **slippery** snow.

The Emperor's Egg

written by Martin Jenkins

illustrated by Jane Chapman

Down at the very bottom of the world, there's a huge island that's almost completely covered in snow and ice. It's called Antarctica, and it's the coldest, windiest place on Earth.

Antarctica

The weather's bad enough there in summer, but in winter it's really terrible. It's hard to imagine anything actually living there.

But wait ...
what's that shape over there?
It can't be.

Yes!

It's a penguin!

It's not just any old penguin
either. It's a male Emperor
penguin (the biggest penguin
in the world), and he's doing a
Very Important Job.

He's taking care of his egg.

He didn't lay it himself, of course.

His mate did that
a few weeks ago.

But very soon
afterward
she turned around
and waddled off
to the sea.

That's where female Emperor penguins
spend most of the winter—swimming about,
getting as fat as they can,
eating as much as they can,
and generally having a very nice time
(as far as you can tell)!

Which leaves the father penguin stuck on the ice with his egg.

Now, the most important thing about egg-sitting is to stop your egg from getting cold.

That means it has to be kept off the ice and out of the wind.

And what better way to do that than to rest it on your feet and tuck it right up under your tummy?

Which is just what the father penguin does.

And that's how he'll stay for two whole months,
until his egg is ready to hatch.

Can you imagine it?
Standing around in the freezing cold
with an egg on your feet
for **two whole** months?

What's more, there's nothing for
the father penguin to eat on land.

And because he's egg-sitting,
he can't go off to the sea to feed.

So that means two whole
months with an egg on your feet **and no dinner!**

Or breakfast

or lunch

or snacks.

I don't know about you

but I'd be **very, very** miserable.

Luckily, the penguins don't seem to mind too
much. They have thick feathers and lots of fat
under their skin to help keep them warm.

And when it gets really cold and windy,
they all snuggle up together and shuffle
over the ice in a great big huddle.

Most of the time, the huddle trundles along
very, very slowly.

But **sometimes,**
when the penguins get to a particularly slippery slope …

they slide down it on their tummies,
pushing themselves along
with their flippers,
always remembering
to take care of their egg—
and trying hard not to bump into each other.

And that's how the father penguin spends
the winter.

Until one day he hears a chip, chip, chip.

His egg is starting to hatch.
It takes a day or so, but finally the egg
cracks right open—

and out pops a penguin chick.

Now the father penguin
has two jobs to do.
He has to keep
the chick warm

and he has to feed it.

But on what? The chick is too small to be taken off to the sea to catch food, and it can't be left behind on the ice.

Well, deep down in the father penguin's throat, there's a pouch where he makes something a little like milk. And that's what he feeds to his hungry chick.

The father penguin can make only enough of the
milky stuff to feed his chick for a couple of weeks.
But just as he's about to run out,
a dot appears on the horizon.

It gets closer
and closer
and yes!

It's mom!

She starts trumpeting **"hello"** and the father penguin starts trumpeting **"hello"** and the chick whistles.

The racket goes on for hours, and it really does sound as if they're extremely pleased to see each other.

As soon as things have calmed down, the mother penguin is sick—right into her chick's mouth!

Yuk,

you may think.

Yum,

thinks the chick,

and gobbles it all down.

It's the mother's turn to take care of the chick now, while the father sets off to the sea for a well-earned meal of his own.

About time, too!

Think Critically

1 How do Emperor penguin fathers take care of their eggs before they hatch?

2 How are Emperor penguin parents the same as a person's family?

3 What did you learn about Emperor penguins that you did not know before?

4 Why do you think the author made some words larger than the others?

Review Vocabulary with a Play

★ STORIES ON STAGE ★

Where Is Buttons?

miserable

remember

police officers

post office

mail carriers

hospital

doctors

librarians

appeared

celebrate

parades

holidays

important

flag

Characters

**Jill,
a dog owner**

**Fire Chief Riggs,
a firefighter**

**Mrs. Larson,
a mail carrier**

**Officer Martinez,
a police officer**

Dr. Jones, a doctor

Miss Han, a librarian

Jill: Fire Chief Riggs, I feel miserable. I can't find Buttons. Have you seen him?

Fire Chief Riggs: I remember seeing him near the police station.

Jill: Thank you! Maybe the police officers have seen him. Can you come with me?

Fire Chief Riggs: I have to get ready for the holiday parade. I will see you later.

Jill: Officer Martinez, I feel miserable. I can't find Buttons. Have you seen him?

Officer Martinez: I remember seeing him near the post office.

Jill: Thank you! Maybe the mail carriers have seen him. Can you come with me?

Officer Martinez: I have to get ready for the holiday parade. I will see you later.

Jill: Mrs. Larson, I feel miserable. I can't find Buttons. Have you seen him?

Mrs. Larson: I remember seeing him near the hospital.

Jill: Thank you! Maybe the doctors have seen him. Can you come with me?

Mrs. Larson: I have to get ready for the holiday parade. I will see you later.

Jill: Dr. Jones, I feel miserable. I can't find Buttons. Have you seen him?

Dr. Jones: I remember seeing him near the library.

Jill: Thank you! Maybe the librarians have seen him. Can you come with me?

Dr. Jones: I have to get ready for the holiday parade. I will see you later.

Jill: Miss Han, I feel terrible. I can't find Buttons. Have you seen him?

Miss Han: Yes, I have. He just appeared at the parade. I'll go with you.

Fire Chief Riggs: Surprise, Jill! We found Buttons.

Officer Martinez: He is helping us celebrate the holiday.

Jill: Can I help? Parades are a fun way to celebrate holidays.

Dr. Jones: I have an important job for you. You can hold the flag.

Miss Han: You and Buttons can lead the parade!

Review Activities

Think and Respond

1. **What are some reasons people celebrate holidays?**

2. **Imagine you have one of the jobs in "Neighborhood Helpers." What would your workday be like?**

3. **How is the animal community in "Tree Story" like the community of people in "Where Is Buttons?"**

4. **How do Emperor penguins work together to care for their babies?**

5. **What does your school community do for you?**

VOCABULARY REVIEW

Riddles

Take turns choosing a word card and making up a riddle about the word. Play until everyone in your group has made a riddle.

What word begins with **p** and means "a line of people celebrating"?

ANSWER: *parade*

LANGUAGE STRUCTURE REVIEW

Give Commands

Play the game "Simon Says."

Choose a leader. The leader gives commands like this.

Simon says, "Take three steps."

Sometimes the leader does *not* say "Simon says" first.

Be sure to do only what Simon says!

Take turns so that everyone can be the leader.

SING ALONG

Exploring We Will Go

Exploring we will go

Through sun and rain and snow.

There's lots to see

For you and me.

So let's get ready and go.

*Sing to the tune of
"The Farmer in the Dell."*

329

Sequence

Story events are usually told in order. This order is called **sequence**. Words like *first, next, then,* and *finally* can help you figure out the sequence.

Read this story.

Big Morning

Mary woke up with a smile. Today, she was starting at her new school! Next, Mary put on her favorite dress. Then, she had breakfast with her family. She was happy to see pancakes on the table. Finally, Mary grabbed her lunch and ran out the door. She didn't want to be late!

This chart shows the sequence of things Mary did.

First	Next	Then	Finally
She woke up.	She got dressed.	She ate breakfast.	She ran out the door.

Try This

▶ Read this story. Then copy the chart below. Complete the chart to show the order in which events happened in the story.

Home Again

Mary got off the bus at home. She was happy about her day at the new school. Next, it was time for dinner. Mary told her parents about the students in her class. Then, it was time to get ready for bed. Mary put on her pajamas. Finally, Mary went to bed. Tomorrow she could see everyone at the new school again.

First	Next	Then	Finally

Vocabulary POWER

Summer Vacation ▼

VOCABULARY

vacation

astronauts

laws

battle

independence

fought

travel

Each summer, we **travel** to the beach for **vacation**.

American soldiers **fought** in a **battle** to keep America free.

Laws tell us what to do. We have to obey the laws.

Astronauts fly high above the earth.

On July 4, we celebrate our country's **independence** and freedom.

Summer Vacation

My family and I spent our summer vacation traveling around Texas. Read about the places we visited.

Johnson Space Center

Astronauts train here in Houston for flights into space.

State Capitol

The laws for the state of Texas are made inside this building in Austin.

The Alamo

An important battle for Texas independence was fought in San Antonio many years ago.

Port Isabel

This lighthouse stands next to the Gulf of Mexico at Port Isabel.

Big Bend National Park

A river called the Rio Grande passes through the park. It marks our country's border with Mexico.

El Paso

This city is near the border between the United States and Mexico.

Palo Duro Canyon State Park

We saw a play about the Old West in an outdoor theater here. Then it was time to go home!

Our vacation was fun. I love to travel!

Vacation Map

El Paso

Big Bend National Park

338

1. What did the family see first?

2. How do you think Big Bend National Park got its name?

3. What facts about Texas did you learn from reading this selection?

4. Which place would you like to visit? Why?

Dallas

Austin

Houston

San Antonio

Gulf of Mexico

Port Isabel

Vocabulary POWER

The Sun, the Moon, and the Silver Baboon ▼

VOCABULARY

bright

evening

gentle

tumbled

tangled

awake

worry

clever

amazed

distant

When the sun goes down, it is **evening**.
The moon shines with a **bright** light.

One bear has its eyes open. It is **awake**.

I see **distant** mountains. The moon shines a **gentle** light on them.

People had to be **clever** to invent the space shuttle. We are **amazed** to see it blast off.

She is **tangled** in the string. Don't **worry**! She can get out.

My dad **tumbled** onto the ground.

The Sun, the Moon, and the Silver Baboon

by Susan Field

Every morning the sun rises and
scatters golden light across the blue sky.

The rooster crows and the birds sing.
A bright new day begins.

Every evening, when the sun goes
to bed, the sky fills with stars, and
the moon lights the land with gentle
silver moonbeams.

343

But one night a star came loose from the sky. Burning bright as a comet, it tumbled to earth and became tangled in the branches of a tree.

"Please help!" called the moon to the animals who were awake. "I cannot leave the sky without all my stars."

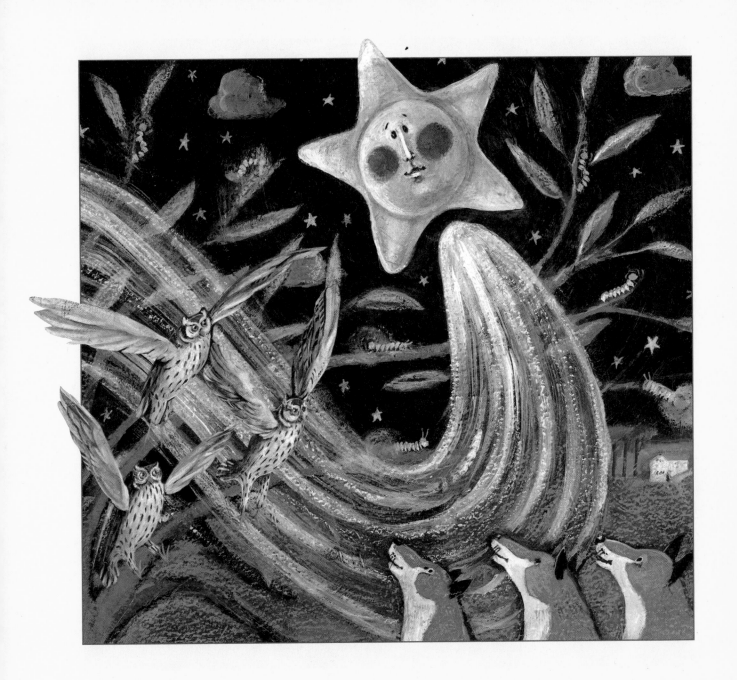

"Don't worry," said the owls, "we will fly up and pull the star from the tree."

"Don't worry," said the insects, "we will crawl up and eat the branches holding it."

"We are clever," said the foxes. "We'll think of something."

But the owls couldn't pull quite hard enough,
the insects couldn't quite eat enough, and the
foxes couldn't think of anything to do.

"Hurry!" said the moon. "It will soon be dawn."

Sure enough, the rooster soon crowed and
the sun came up. Now all the animals were
awake and amazed to find the sun, the
moon, and the stars all together in the sky.

"Help me!" the star called to them. "My tail
is caught and I cannot get free."

"Don't worry," said the giraffes, "we are tall. We will lift you out of the tree."

"Don't worry," said the elephants, "we are strong. We will shake you out."

"Ha! Ha! Ha!" laughed the hyenas, who were no help at all.

But the giraffes weren't quite tall enough,
the elephants weren't quite strong enough,
and the hyenas just couldn't stop laughing.

Soon all the animals were talking and
arguing about what to do next. The noise
was tremendous.

The uproar could be heard even in
the distant mountains, where a
brown baboon was sleeping.

His ears began to twitch and his sleepy
eyes slowly opened. He yawned, stretched,
and then padded down the mountain to
find out what all the fuss was about.

The animals were all so busy arguing that
they didn't notice the brown baboon. He took
one look at the star in the tree and saw what
needed to be done.

Like a shadow he slipped through the noisy
crowd and climbed the tree. His quick, nimble
fingers loosened the tangled tail, and soon
the star was free.

Up, up, up the star flew, high into the sky.

"Thank you!" said the moon. "Now the night can end." And the moon gave the baboon a coat as silver as moonlight.

"Thank you!" said the sun. "Now the day can begin." And the sun gave the baboon a face as warm as sunlight.

Now the baboon is no longer brown. From the tip of his new crimson nose to the end of his fine silver tail, he shines as bright as any star.

Think Critically

1. How does the baboon help the star?

2. What parts of this story make it a folktale?

3. Why do you think people made up a folktale about the silver baboon?

4. What other folktales do you know?

Vocabulary POWER

First Flight ▼

VOCABULARY

flew

airplane

helicopter

flight

built

machine

steam

engine

pilot

This **airplane** is taking a long **flight**.

The **pilot** **flew** the airplane.

A **helicopter** goes straight up when it takes off.

This **engine** was **built** for a big airplane.

This old train uses **steam** to run its engine.

The farmer uses this **machine** to gather his crops.

First Flight

When Wilbur and Orville Wright were children, they loved things that flew. Years later, they would be the first people to fly an airplane.

Wilbur Wright, age 12

Orville Wright, age 8

Wilbur and Orville Wright were brothers who lived in Dayton, Ohio. One day their father gave them a toy that would change their lives—and ours. It was called a helicopter, but it was really just a propeller.

The boys were very excited about the helicopter toy. They tried to make and fly bigger ones like it. From that time on, they were always interested in flight.

propeller

When the Wright brothers grew up, they read about people who were building flying machines. One man had built a flying machine that used a steam engine to turn its propellers, but there were problems. No one knew how to take off, turn around, or come back down.

The Wright brothers began to try different kinds of wings that might lift a flying machine into the air. They made many gliders to test their wings. Gliders are airplanes without engines. The brothers flew them like kites. They discovered that a glider with two sets of wings worked well. Now they needed a glider big enough to carry a person.

The Wright brothers also needed a place with strong, steady winds. They decided that Kitty Hawk, North Carolina, would be the best place. For several years, they traveled to Kitty Hawk to test different gliders.

Finally, they made a glider that could lift a person into the air. The person could also bring it back down to the ground. Now all the brothers had to do was to build an engine.

At last, on December 17, 1903, the Wright brothers were ready to try their flying machine. Orville was chosen to be the pilot. The airplane sped down the runway. Suddenly it rose into the air!

That first flight lasted only twelve seconds, but it showed the world that people can fly. That's why we will always remember the Wright brothers.

How People Go

bus

car

People use cars and buses to travel over land.

plane

People can travel
through the air
in a plane.

People travel under the ground in subways.

subway

boat

Boats let people travel over water.

Think Critically

1. What things did the Wright brothers have to figure out to invent the first airplane?

2. Why did the Wright brothers need to find a place with strong winds?

3. What things do you know that fly?

4. What other ways do people travel?

Vocabulary POWER

The Night of the Stars ▼

VOCABULARY

horrible

lamp

peak

disappear

conversation

poked

flickered

The top of a mountain is called the **peak**.

People got very wet during the **horrible** rainstorm.

The girls are having a **conversation** about school.

The campers use a **lamp** to have light at night. When they turn off the lamp, the light will **disappear**.

The baker **poked** holes in the dough with her fingers.

The light from the fireworks **flickered** on and off.

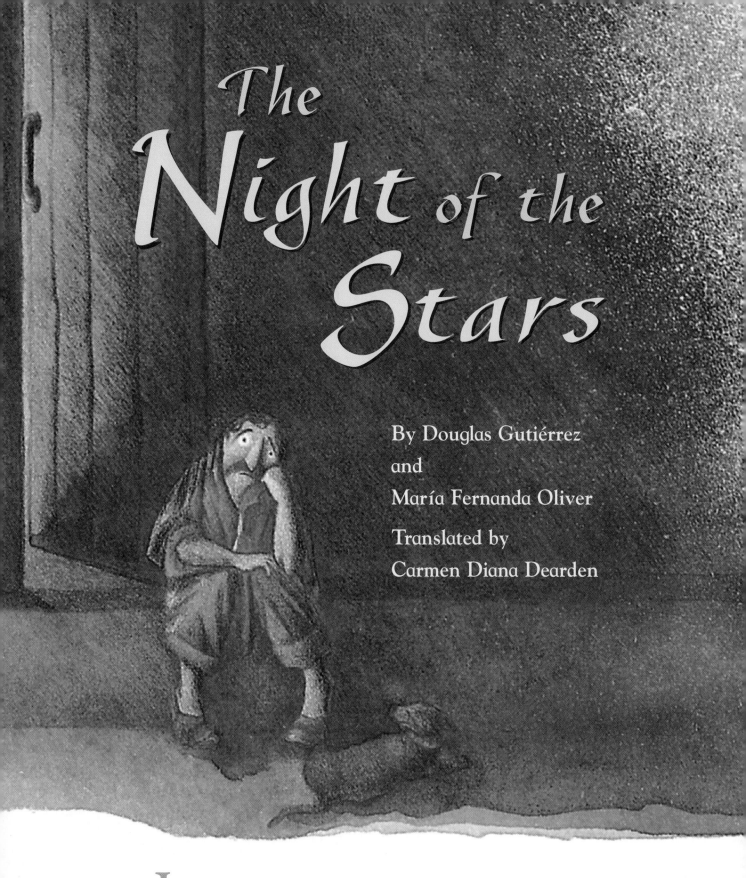

The Night of the Stars

By Douglas Gutiérrez
and
María Fernanda Oliver

Translated by
Carmen Diana Dearden

Long, long ago, in a town that was neither near
nor far, there lived a man who did not like the night.

During the day, in the sunlight, he worked weaving baskets, watching over his animals and watering his vegetables.

Often he would sing. But as soon as the sun set behind the mountain, this man who did not like the night would become sad, for his world suddenly turned gray, dark and black.

"Night again! Horrible night!" he would cry out.

He would then pick up his baskets, light his lamp and shut himself up in his house.

Sometimes he would look out the window, but there was nothing to see in the dark sky. So he would put out his lamp and go to bed.

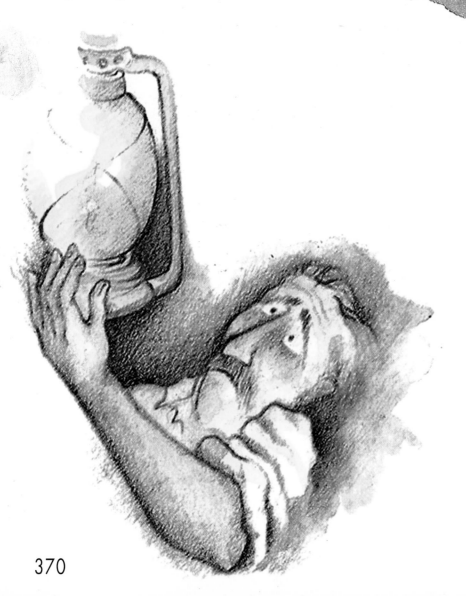

One day, at sunset, the man went to the
mountain. Night was beginning to cover the blue sky.

The man climbed to the highest peak and
shouted:

"Please, night. Stop!"

And the night did stop for a moment.

"What is it?" she asked in a soft deep voice.

"Night, I don't like you. When you come, the
light goes away and the colors disappear. Only the
darkness remains."

"You're right," answered the night. "It is so."

"Tell me, where do you take the light?" asked the man.

"It hides behind me, and I cannot do anything about it," replied the night. "I'm very sorry."

The night finished stretching and covered the world with darkness.

The man came down from the mountain and went to bed.

But he could not sleep.

Nor during the next day could he work. All he could think about was his conversation with the night. And in the afternoon, when the light began to disappear again, he said to himself: "I know what to do."

Once more he went to the mountain. The night was like an immense awning, covering all things. When at last he reached the highest point on the mountain, the man stood on his tiptoes, and with his finger poked a hole in the black sky.

A pinprick of light flickered through the hole.

The man who did not like the night was delighted.

He poked holes all over the sky.

Here, there, everywhere, and all over the sky little points of light appeared.

Amazed now at what he could do, the man made a fist and punched it through the darkness.

A large hole opened up, and a huge round light, almost like a grapefruit, shone through.

All the escaping light cast a brilliant glow at the base of the mountain and lit up everything below . . . the fields, the street, the houses.

Everything.

That night, no one in the town slept.

And ever since then, the night is full of lights, and people everywhere can stay up late . . . looking at the moon and the stars.

Think Critically

❶ What does the man do to the night sky?

❷ What parts of the story help you know it is a fantasy?

❸ Why do you think the man did not like the night?

❹ Do you like daytime or nighttime better? Why?

Review Vocabulary with a Play

★ STORIES ON STAGE ★

The Three Billy Goats Gruff

Review

VOCABULARY

conversation

distant

horrible

built

worry

clever

amazed

travel

evening

Characters

Little Billy Goat Gruff

Big Billy Goat Gruff

Great Big Billy Goat Gruff

Troll

Narrator

377

Narrator: Once upon a time there were three billy goats. They lived on one side of a bridge. On the other side was a hill with lots of grass. One day they had a conversation.

Little Billy Goat Gruff: I want to cross that bridge and eat the grass on that distant hill.

Big Billy Goat Gruff: I do, too. But the horrible troll who built the bridge would eat us.

Great Big Billy Goat Gruff: You don't need to worry about the troll. I have a clever plan.

Narrator: Great Big Billy Goat Gruff told the others his plan. They were amazed at how clever he was.

Narrator: Little Billy Goat Gruff was the first to try to travel across the bridge.

Troll: WHO'S THAT WALKING ACROSS MY BRIDGE?

Little Billy Goat Gruff: It is Little Billy Goat Gruff.

Troll: No one can cross my bridge! Wait right there. I am coming to eat you.

Little Billy Goat Gruff: Oh, no. Don't eat me. Wait for the next billy goat. He is much bigger than I am.

Troll: Well, I AM very hungry, so you may cross the bridge.

Narrator: Big Billy Goat Gruff was the next to try to travel across the bridge.

Troll: WHO'S THAT WALKING ACROSS MY BRIDGE?

Big Billy Goat Gruff: It is Big Billy Goat Gruff.

Troll: No one can cross my bridge! Wait right there. I am coming to eat you.

Big Billy Goat Gruff: Oh, no. Don't eat me. Wait for the next billy goat. He is much bigger than I am.

Troll: Well, I AM very hungry, so you may cross the bridge.

Narrator: Great Big Billy Goat Gruff was the last to try to travel across the bridge.

Troll: WHO'S THAT WALKING ACROSS MY BRIDGE?

Great Big Billy Goat Gruff: It is Great Big Billy Goat Gruff.

Troll: No one can cross my bridge! Wait right there. I am coming to eat you.

Great Big Billy Goat Gruff: Come and try to eat me, Troll!

Narrator: When the angry troll got on the bridge, he just looked at Great Big Billy Goat Gruff.

Troll: You are a very big billy goat!

Great Big Billy Goat Gruff: Yes, I am. Do you want to fight with me?

Troll: No. You are much too big for me to eat. I will let you cross.

Narrator: The troll was so scared that he jumped off the bridge and never came back. From that day on, the billy goats lived on the grassy hill. They ate grass from morning until evening.

Little Billy Goat Gruff: The grass on this hill is very good.

Big Billy Goat Gruff: There is enough for us to eat for a long time.

Great Big Billy Goat Gruff: I'm glad the troll was so hungry!

383

Review Activities

Think and Respond

1. What kinds of places does the family visit in "Summer Vacation"?

2. Why is the silver baboon rewarded?

3. How did the Wright brothers change the way people travel?

4. How are "The Sun, the Moon, and the Silver Baboon" and "The Night of the Stars" alike?

5. How do the billy goats trick the troll?

VOCABULARY REVIEW

Word Sort

Write the Vocabulary words in a chart like the one below.

Nouns	Verbs	Describing Words
	built	

Compare your chart with a friend's chart. Talk about why you put each word in the group you did.

LANGUAGE STRUCTURE REVIEW

Talk About a Routine

You can make a flip book to tell about one of your routines.

When I get home from school, I feed my fish.

1. Think about routines that you have. Choose one.

2. Draw pictures that show the order you do things. Put your pictures together to make a flip book.

3. Share your flip book with the class. Tell about your routine as you flip the pages.

Glossary

What Is a Glossary?

A glossary is like a small dictionary. You can use it when you need to know what a word means. You can look up the word and read it in a sentence. Some words have a picture to help you.

as•tro•nauts [as′trə•nôts] People who travel in space: **The spacecraft is carrying three *astronauts* to the moon.** astronaut

A

af•ter•noon [af′tər•nōōn′] The part of the day between noon and evening: **The baby takes a nap in the *afternoon.***

air•plane [âr′plān′] A machine that carries people through the air: **We watched the *airplane* flying high in the sky.**

a•mazed [ə•māzd′] Filled with wonder: **She was *amazed* by how fast the horse ran.** amaze, amazing

an•cient [ān′shənt] From long ago: **The *ancient* tribe left pictures of animals on the cave wall.**

as•tro•nauts [as′trə•nôts] People who travel in space: **The spacecraft is carrying three *astronauts* to the moon.** astronaut

a•wake [ə•wāk′] Not asleep: **He is *awake* early every morning.**

B

bark [bärk] The covering of a tree: **The *bark* of a birch tree peels off easily.**

barn [bärn] A farm building that is a place for cows and horses to live in: **The farmer feeds his horses in the *barn.***

bat•tle [bat′əl] A fight or struggle: **Dad won the *battle* to lose his extra weight.**

bikes [bīks] A shorter name for *bicycles*, machines with two wheels and a seat. A rider moves a bike with pedals and steers it with a handlebar: **Thomas and Carlos ride their *bikes* to school.**

blan•ket [blang′kit] A large piece of soft cloth used as a cover in bed: **Mother covered me with a *blanket* and kissed me good night.**

blue [blōō] Sad or discouraged: **Julian felt *blue* when he lost his backpack.**

airplane

astronauts

barn

bikes

building

celebrate

crumbled

book•store [bŏŏk′stôr] A store that sells books and other things to read: **The** *bookstore* **sells books, magazines, newspapers, and greeting cards.**

bright [brīt] Giving off a lot of light: **The stars are** *bright* **tonight.**

build•ing [bil′ding] A structure, such as a house or a barn: **The library is the newest** *building* **in our town.**

C

car•ry [kar′ē] To move something from one place to another: **I will** *carry* **my dirty dishes to the sink.**

cel•e•brate [sel′ə•brāt] To honor a special person or day: **We** *celebrate* **the Fourth of July in the United States.**

clev•er [klev′ər] Good at learning and at solving problems: **The girl is a** *clever* **student.**

com•put•ers [kəm•pyŏŏ′tərz] Machines that can find, save, and put together information: **Students use** *computers* **to help them with schoolwork.**

con•ver•sa•tion [kän′vər•sā′shən] A talk: **The teacher and the principal had a** *conversation* **in the hallway.**

coun•try [kun′trē] A land with its own people and government: **Mexico is a** *country* **in North America.**

cre•ate [krē•āt′] To make something new: **Our class will** *create* **pictures that go with the story.**

crum•bled [krum′bəld] Broke into crumbs, or tiny pieces: **The cookie** *crumbled* **into little bits in the baby's hand.** crumble, crumbling

cure [kyŏŏr] To make well: **The medicine will** *cure* **the boy's sickness.**

D

dam [dam] A wall built to hold back the water of a stream or river: **Behind the *dam* the river has formed a lake.**

damp [damp] A little bit wet: **The *damp* air in the deep woods felt cold.**

des·ert [dez′ərt] A very dry place where most kinds of plants will not grow: **The travelers filled their water bottles before crossing the *desert.***

de·signs [di•zīnz′] Patterns made up of shapes and colors: **The pink and white tiles made pretty *designs* on the bathroom floor.** design

di·a·gram [dī′ə•gram′] A drawing that shows the parts of something: **Jordan drew a *diagram* showing where everything is in his bedroom.** *syn.* plan

dis·ap·pear [dis•ə•pir′] To go out of sight: **The squirrels run up the tree and *disappear* into a hole.**

dis·cov·ered [dis•kuv′ərd] Found or learned about something: **Ellen *discovered* the lost kitten hiding in a basket.** discover, discovering

dis·tant [dis′tənt] Far away: **We saw a *distant* ship on the horizon.**

doc·tors [dok′tərz] People trained to help sick people get well: **The *doctors* helped Mr. Johnson get better when he was sick.** doctor

E

ed·i·tor [ed′i•tər] A person who helps a writer make his or her work better: **The *editor* helped the writer make his book the best it could be.**

en·gine [en′jin] A machine with parts that work together to make something work or move: **The *engine* must be fixed before we can drive the car.**

eve·ning [ēv′ning] The part of the day between afternoon and night: **We eat dinner in the *evening.***

ex·am·ine [ig•zam′in] To look at closely and carefully: **The dentist will *examine* the children's teeth.**

dam

desert

doctors

family

fence

flag

flowerpot

F

fac·to·ries [fak'tər•ēz] Buildings in which things are made or put together with machines: **Many people work at the *factories* in our city.** factory

fam·i·ly [fam'ə•lē *or* fam'lē] A group of people who live together: **This apartment has room for a *family* of four people.**

fa·vor·ite [fā'vər•it] Liked best of all: **What is your *favorite* sport?**

feed [fēd] To give food to: **We *feed* our dog in the morning and in the evening.**

fence [fens] A kind of open wall built outdoors: **Our neighbors put a *fence* around their yard to keep their puppy safe.**

field [fēld] A large piece of land with few or no trees: **The *field* behind the barn is covered with grass and flowers.**

flag [flag] A piece of cloth with colors and designs that represents a country: **The *flag* of the United States has stars and stripes and is red, white, and blue.**

flow·er·pot [flou'ər•pot] A pot filled with dirt and used for growing plants: **Daniel set a *flowerpot* on the front steps.**

food [fo͞od] Anything that is eaten by animals or people to help them grow and live: **Lucy put *food* in her dog's bowl.**

G

gen·tle [jen'təl] Quiet or kind: **The woman spoke with a *gentle* voice to the children.**

grow [grō] To get bigger in size: **The tree will *grow* to become very tall.**

H

hatch [hach] To come out of an egg: **Chicks *hatch* from eggs.**

health•y [hel′thē] Having good health: **The Monroe family has three *healthy* children.**

heat [hēt] Warmth: **The campers felt the *heat* from the campfire.**

hel•i•cop•ter [hel′ə•kop•tər] An aircraft without wings that has a rotor on top: **A *helicopter* can fly in any direction.**

high•ways [hī′wāz] Main roads used by fast-moving cars and trucks: **We will get there faster if we travel on the *highways.***

his•to•ry [his′tə•rē] The story of what has happened to a person or a country in the past: **Many students enjoy learning the *history* of their country.**

hol•i•days [hol′ə•dāz] Special days on which people do not go to school or work: **We do not get mail on most *holidays.*** holiday

hos•pi•tal [hos′pi•təl] A building in which injured or sick people are cared for: **The injured man was taken to the *hospital.***

I

il•lus•trates [il′ə•strāts′] Makes pictures to go with a story: **This artist *illustrates* children's books.** illustrate, illustrating

in•de•pen•dence [in•di•pen′dəns] Freedom from being told by others what to do: **The colonists won their *independence* from the king.**

in•for•ma•tion [in•fər•mā′shən] Facts: **The library has books with *information* about many things.**

is•land [ī′lənd] Land that has water all around it: **There were sandy beaches all around the *island.***

hatch

helicopter

highways

island

ladder

lightning

medicine

L

lad•der [lad′ər] A set of steps attached to two long pieces of wood or metal, used for climbing to reach something: **We climbed a *ladder* to reach the attic.**

laws [lôz] Rules made by a state or country for all the people who live there to follow: **We must follow the *laws* to live safely.** law

li•brar•i•ans [lī•brâr′ē•ənz] People trained in library work: **Our library has *librarians* to help people find and check out books.** librarian

light•ning [līt′ning] A sudden flash of light in the sky during a storm: **Our dog did not like the *lightning* during the storm.**

M

ma•chine [mə•shēn′] An object with moving parts that does some kind of work: **You can save a lot of time by using a washing *machine* to wash clothes.**

mail car•ri•ers [māl kar′ē•ərz] People who carry and give out mail: **Two *mail carriers* work in my neighborhood.** mail carrier

med•i•cine [med′ə•sən] Something given to sick people or animals to help them get well: **Rudy's mother gave him *medicine* when he had a cold.**

mis•er•a•ble [miz′ər•ə•bəl] Very unhappy or sick: **The child's sore throat made him feel *miserable*.**

mis•take [mis•tāk′] An error: **Sam made a *mistake* on the spelling test today.**

mound [mound] A small hill or pile of earth or rocks: **The rabbit left a *mound* of dirt where it had been digging.**

N

neigh·bor·hood [nā′bər•hŏŏd] A small part of a city or town where people live: **Many families live in our *neighborhood.***

nurs·es [nûrs′əz] People who help doctors care for people: **The *nurses* took care of the new babies in the hospital.** nurse

P

paint [pānt] A colored liquid that is brushed onto something to color it: **Da-Un brushed green *paint* onto his clay bowl.**

pa·rades [pə•rādz′] Groups of people marching together down a street: **We saw two *parades* on Memorial Day.** parade

par·ty [pär′tē] A special event at which people have a good time together: **Mike invited his friends to a *party* at his home.**

pic·nics [pik′niks] Meals that people share outdoors: **During the summer, we had several *picnics* at the park.** picnic

pic·tures [pik′chərz] Paintings, drawings, or photographs that show a scene, person, object, or design: **Shelby has three *pictures* of the Rocky Mountains on her wall.** picture

piece [pēs] A part of something: **We each ate a *piece* of pizza for lunch.**

pi·lot [pī′lət] The person who flies an airplane or helicopter: **The *pilot* landed the plane safely.**

po·lice of·fi·cers [pə•lēs′ ôf′ə•sərz] People who protect other people and make sure people follow laws: **Our city has many *police officers* to keep us safe.** police officer

porch [pôrch] A covered structure at the entrance to a building: **We waited on the *porch* until the rain stopped.**

party

pilot

police officers

393

post of·fice [pōst ôf′is] A place where mail is taken and stamps are sold: **I went to the *post office* to mail my letters.**

pot·ter·y [pot′ər•ē] Objects such as dishes and pots made from clay and hardened by heat: **This beautiful *pottery* was made by a Native American woman.**

pouch [pouch] A pocket: **The kangaroo carries its young in a *pouch*.**

pre·dict [pri•dikt′] To figure out what will happen before it does: **The farmer could *predict* when it would rain.**

pre·pare [pri•pâr′] To get ready: **Rita is packing clothes to *prepare* for her trip to Chile.**

prod·ucts [prod′əkts] Things that are grown or made: **The factory makes many *products* used for sports.** product

R

railroad

rail·road [rāl′rōd] The trains and tracks that connect cities for travel: **When the *railroad* came to our town, many people moved here.**

red [red] The bright color of a ripe tomato: **Red is the color used for STOP signs.**

re·mem·ber [ri•mem′bər] To find in your mind something from the past: **I never can *remember* telephone numbers.**

re·search [ri•sûrch′ or rē′sûrch] Careful study: **The writer did a lot of *research* about cats before writing about them.**

ride [rīd] To travel in or on something: **Cora will *ride* her bike to the park.**

red

ride

S

sci•en•tists [sī'ən•tists] People whose job it is to learn about things: **The *scientists* spent hours studying the movements of the ants.** scientist

sea [sē] The salt water that covers most of the earth: **Many kinds of animals live in the *sea*.** *syn.* ocean

sea

share [shâr] To let everyone have some: **We will cut six pieces and *share* the pie.**

shine [shīn] To give off light: **The sun will *shine* all day.**

show•er [shou'ər] A light fall of rain: **The dry lawn looked greener after the *shower*.**

sketch [skech] A quick drawing without details: **The artist made a quick *sketch* of the cat.**

slip•per•y [slip'ər•ē] Hard to stand on without sliding: **The icy sidewalk was *slippery*.**

sketch

snug•gle [snug'əl] To hold close or cuddle: **I *snuggle* with Mom when we read a book.**

soil [soil] The ground in which plants grow: **Jacob planted pumpkin seeds in the rich *soil*.** *syns.* dirt, earth

spin [spin] To make something turn quickly: **The store clerk will *spin* the top to show how it works.**

sprout•ed [sprout'əd] Began to grow: **Becky watched the bean seed every day until it *sprouted*.** sprout, sprouting

steam [stēm] Water that has become a gas: **When water boils, it becomes *steam*.**

sprouted

T

tan·gled [tang'gəld] Twisted: **The ropes became *tangled.*** tangle

teams [tēmz] Groups of people who work or play together: **The two basketball *teams* had played against each other before.** team

teams

ter·ri·ble [ter'ə•bəl] Very bad: **We had a *terrible* storm last night.**

throat [thrōt] The front part of the neck under the chin: **This collar is too tight around my *throat.***

trem·ble [trem'bəl] To shake because of fear or cold: **My fingers *tremble* when I feel really cold.**

tum·bled [tum'bəld] Fell down or rolled about: **The children *tumbled* on the lawn.** tumble, tumbling

tremble

U

um·brel·las [um•brel'əz] Little shelters used to keep off rain or sun: **We put up our *umbrellas* when it started to rain.** umbrella

W

wad·dled [wod'əld] Swayed from side to side in walking: **The duck *waddled* over to the pond.** waddle, waddling

weath·er [weth'ər] What it is like outside: **Ji-Young will wear a sweater in this cool *weather.***

wor·ry [wûr'ē] To feel that something bad will happen or has happened: **Mom will *worry* if I don't call her.**

umbrellas

Index *of* Titles *and* Authors

Acknowledgments

For permission to reprint copyrighted material, grateful acknowledgment is made to the following sources:

Candlewick Press Inc., Cambridge, MA: Little Lumpty by Miko Imai. Copyright © 1994 by Miko Imai.

Candlewick Press Inc., Cambridge, MA, on behalf of Walker Books Ltd., London: From *The Emperor's Egg* by Martin Jenkins, illustrated by Jane Chapman. Text © 1999 by Martin Jenkins; illustrations © 1999 by Jane Chapman.

Children's Book Press: "Daily Shower" from *From the Bellybutton of the Moon and Other Summer Poems* by Francisco X. Alarcón. Text copyright © 1998 by Francisco X. Alarcón.

CLICK Magazine: "Tree Story" from *Click* Magazine, Vol. 2, No. 8. Text copyright © 1999 by Carus Publishing Company.

Alan and Lea Daniel: Illustrations by Alan and Lea Daniel from "Tree Story" in *Click* Magazine, October 1999.

HarperCollins Publishers: "First Snow" from *A Pocketful of Poems* by Marie Louise Allen. Text copyright © 1957 by Marie Allen Howarth. *Fran's Flower* by Lisa Bruce, illustrated by Rosalind Beardshaw. Text copyright © 1999 by Lisa Bruce; illustrations copyright © 1999 by Rosalind Beardshaw. *The Sun, the Moon, and the Silver Baboon* by Susan Field. Copyright © 1993 by Susan Field. "The Story" from *Frog and Toad Are Friends* by Arnold Lobel. Copyright © 1970 by Arnold Lobel.

Kane/Miller Book Publishers: The Night of the Stars by Douglas Gutiérrez, illustrated by María Fernanda Oliver. Published in the United States by Kane/Miller Book Publishers, 1988.

Karen S. Solomon: "Change in the Weather" by Ilo Orleans.

Photo Credits

Page Placement Key:

(t)-top, (b)-bottom, (c)-center, (l)-left, (r)-right, (fg)-foreground, (bg)-background, (I)-inset

18 (t) William Gottlieb/Corbis; (b) Corbis; 19 (t) Steve Raymer/Corbis; (bl) RNT Productions/Corbis; (br) Corbis; 38 (t) Ariel Skelley/Corbis; (b) Brooklyn Production/Corbis; (t) Corbis; 39 (bl) Steve Chenn/Corbis; (br) Norbert Schafer/Corbis; 48 (t) Harcourt; (b) Norbert Schafer/Corbis; 49 (t) Richard Huthcings/Corbis; (bl) Rick Gomez/Corbis; (br) Tom Stewart/Corbis; 40-45 Ken Kinzie/Harcourt; 46 Harcourt Index; 46-47 (bg) Ken Kinzie/Harcourt; 47 (r) Harcourt; 64 (t) Corbis; (b) Bob Kirst/Corbis; 65 (tr) Talph A. Clevenger/Corbis; (tl) Ariel Skelley/Corbis; (bl) Kelly/Mooney Photography/Corbis; (br) Rick Meyer.Corbis; 66 (t) Ken Kinzie/Harcourt; (b) [left to right] Harcourt Index, Harcourt, SW Productions/Getty Images, Doug Berry/Corbis, Ken Kinzie/Harcourt, Massis J. Boujikian/Corbis; 67 (tl) Ken Kinzie; (tr, b) Harcourt Index; (c) Harcourt; 68 (tl) Ken Kinzie/Harcourt; (cr) Harcourt; (b) SW Productions/Getty Images; 69 (tl) Ken Kinzie/Harcourt; (tr) Doug Berry/Corbis; (cr) Debra Cohn-Orbach/Index Stock Imagery; (b) Chinch Gryniewicz/Ecoscene/Corbis; 70 (tl, tr) Ken Kinzie/Harcourt; (b) Jim Cummins/Taxi/Getty Images; 71 (t) Massis J. Boujikian/Corbis; Ken Kinzie/Harcourt;86 (t) Harcourt; (b) Dimitri Lundt/Corbis; 87 (tl,bl,br) Harcourt; (tl) William Gottlieb/Corbis; 96 (t) Tom & Dee McCarthy/Corbis; (b) Tim Pannell/Corbis; 97 (tr,bl,br) Harcourt; (tl) Vince Streano/Corbis; 98 Adamsmith Productions/Corbis; 99 (b) Syracuse Newspapers/The Image Works; (t) Natalie Forbes/Corbis; 100 (b) John Boykin/Index Stock Imagery/PictureQuest; (t) Geostock/PhotoDisc/PictureQuest; 101 (l) Steve Dunwell/The Image Bank/ Getty Images; (r) Gary Moon Photography; 102-103 (bg) David Hanson/Stone/ Getty Images; 102 (t) Inc. Chuck Kuhn Photography/The Image Bank/Getty Images; 103 (tl) Gary Moon Photography; (tr) Corbis; (cl) Gehl Company/Corbis; (cr) Syracuse Newspapers/The Image Bank;104 (t) Kurt tier/Corbis; (b) Joel Katz/Corbis; 105 (tl) Tom Stewart/Corbis; (tr) Lawrence Manning/Corbis; (br) Royalty Free/Corbis; (bl) Ariel Skelley/Corbis; 106-117 Rick Friedman; 118 (t) Dave G. Houser/Corbis; (b) Harcourt; 119 (tl,bl,br) Harcourt; (tr) Michael Krasowitz/Taxi/Getty Images; 140-147 Ken Kinzie/Harcourt;154-155 Harcourt; 156-157 (bg) El Paso County Historical Society; 157 (c) El Paso Public Library; 158 El Paso County Historical Society; 159 Gerald French/Corbis; 160 (tl) Chad Ehlers/The Image Bank/Getty Images; (cl) Douglas Stone/Corbis; (bl) Paul A. Sounders/Corbis; 160-161 (fg) C. E. Mitchell/Black Star; 162 (b) Amos Morgan.PhotoDisc/PictureQuest; (t) Harcourt; 163 (tl) Carl & Ann Purcell/Corbis; (br) Jim McDonald/Corbis; (bl) Harcourt; (tr) AFP/Corbis;165 (cr) Ken Kinzie/Harcourt; (t) Thomas Wiewandt/Taxi/Getty Images; 166 (cl) Ken Kinzie/ Harcourt; (t) Harcourt; 167 (cr) Ken Kinzie/Harcourt; (t) Harcourt; 168 (cr) Ken Kinzie/Harcourt; (bg) Peter Johnson/Corbis; 169 Harcourt; 170 (t,b) Corbis; 171 (tl,tr,br) Harcourt; (bl) Corbis;172-173 Weronica Ankarorn/Harcourt; 174, 175 Ken Kinzie/Harcourt, Kinzie/Harcourt; 179 Weronica Ankarorn/Harcourt; 180 (t) Bruce Coleman; (c) Tony Savino/The Image Works; 181 (t) Bob Strong/The Image Works; (c) Ralph H. Wetmore II/Stone/Getty Images; 182 Harcourt; 183 (tl,tr,bl) Harcourt; (br) Wartenberg/Picture Press/Corbis; 216 (t) Corbis; (b) Harcourt; 217 (t) Harcourt; (b) Charles Gupton/Corbis; 218-223 Ken Kinzie/Harcourt; 224 (t) Harcourt; (b) James Marshall/Corbis; 225 (br,bl) Harcourt; (tl) Ariel Skelley/Corbis; (tr) LWA-Stephen Welstead/Corbis; 240 (b) Corbis; (t) James A. Sugar/Corbis; 241 (tl,tr,br) Harcourt; (br) Corbis; 242 (t) Museum of Indian Arts and Culture/Laboratory of Anthropology; (b) Maurice Eby/Museum of New Mexico; 242-243 (bg) Claire Rydell/Index Stock Imagery; 244 (b) Harcourt; (tr) Wyatt Davis/Museum of New Mexico; 244-245 (c) Museum of Indian Arts and Culture/Laboratory of Anthropology; 244-245 (bg) Cornell Capa/TimePix; 246 (bl) Museum of Indian Arts and Culture/Laboratory of Anthropology; (b) T. Harmon Parkhurst/Museum of New Mexico; (tr) Wyatt Davis/ Museum of New Mexico; 246 (t) Corbis; (b) Harcourt; 247 (tl) Reuters NewMedia/Corbis; (tr) David Buffington/PhotoDisc/PictureQuest; (bl) harcourt; (br) Ed Bock/Corbis; 268 (t) Morton Beebe/Corbis; (b) Ariel Skelley/Corbis; 269 (br) Museum of the City of New York/Corbis; (tr, bl) Harcourt; 271 (tl, c) Ken Kinzie; 272 (t) Pennsylvania Historical Society/Harcourt; (cr) Joseph Sohm; Visions of America/Corbis; (b) Phil Kramer Photographers, Inc.; (bg) Kathy Tarantola/Index Stock Imagery; 274-275 (bg) Harcourt; 275 (fg,b,tl) Harcourt; (tr) Oscar White/Corbis; (cl) Independence National Historical Park; (cr) Bettmann/Corbis; 276 (t) Hisham Ibrahim/Corbis; (bg) EyeWire/Getty Images; 277 (tr) Harcourt; (br) Peter Burian/Corbis; 278 (t,b) Harcourt; 279 (tl) Getty Images; (bl) Corbis; (tr) Mug Shots/Corbis; (br) Michael Heron/Corbis; 280 Larry Kolvoord/The Image Works; 281 (b) Henry Diltz/Corbis; (c) Aneal Vohra/Index Stock Imagery; 282 (b) Peter Hvizdak/The Image Works; (c) Harcourt; 283 (cr) corbisstockmarket.com/Corbis; (b) Bow Rowan; Progressive Image/ Corbis; (cl) Harcourt; 284 (c) Charles Shoffner/Index Stock Imagery/PictureQuest; (c) Greg Kinch/Black Star/Harcourt; 285 (tl) Harcourt; (tcl) Peter Hvizdak/the Image Works; (tc) Henry Diltz/Corbis; (cr) Reed Kaestner/Corbis; (br) Gaetano/Corbis; (cl) Harcourt; (c) Scott T. Smith/Corbis; 286 (t.b) Harcourt; 287 (tl) Jose Luis Pelaez, Inc./Corbis; (tr) Harcourt; (bl) Wolfgang Kaehler/Corbis; (br) Paul Almasy/Corbis; 288 (bl) Stephen Dalton/Animals Animals; (br) Tom Ulrich/Visuals Unlimited; 289 (bl) Stephen J. Lang/Visuals Unlimited; 289 (br) Dwight R. Kuhn/Visuals Unlimited; 290 David T. Roberts/Photo Research; 291 (tl) John Serrao/Visuals Unlimited; (c) William J. Webber/Visuals Unlimited; 292 (tl) Bill Beatty/Visuals Unlimited; (tr) Bill Beatty/Visuals Unlimited; 292 Gerald & Buff Corsi/Visuals Unlimited; 294 (t) Harcourt; (b) Gallo Images/Corbis; 295 (t) Corbis; (tr) Gallo Images/Corbis; (bl) John Conrad/Corbis; (br) Corbis; 318-325 Ken Kinzie/Harcourt; 332 (t) Douglas Peebles/Corbis; (b) Harcourt; 333 (bl) Ted Spiegel/Corbis; (t) Corbis; (br) Phil Schermeister/Corbis; 334 (b) Weronica Ankarorn/Harcourt; 335 (t) NASA/ Harcourt; (b) L. Clarke/Corbis; 336 (t) D Boone/Corbis; (c) Buddy Mays/Travel Stock Photography; (b) Bruce Coleman, Inc.; 337 (t) Laurence Parent Photography; (c) Bob Daemmrich/The Image Work; (b) Weronica Ankarorn/Harcourt; 340 (t) Harcourt; (b) Dan Guravich/Corbis; 341 (tl,tr) Harcourt; (bl) RF/Corbis; (br) Ed Bock/Corbis; 356 (t) Firefly Productions/Corbis; (b) Corbis; 357 (tl) Lowell Georgia/Corbis; (tr) John Olson/Corbis; (br) Harcourt; (bl) Dorothy Burrows; Eye Ubiquitous/Corbis; 358 Bettman/Corbis; 359 (t) Henry Ford Museum & Greenfield Village; (b) Harcourt; 360 (b) Corbis; 361 (t) Bettmann/Corbis; 363 (t) Bettmann/Corbis; (cr) Library of Congress; 364 (t) Richard T. Nowitz/Corbis; 365 (c) Corbis; (b) William A. Bake/Corbis; 364 (c) Paul Duckworth, Jr./Camerique International; (b) Kent Meireis/The Image Works; 365 (t) Harcourt; (c) Harcourt; (b) Pierre DuCharme/Reuters NewMedia Inc./Corbis; 366 Harcourt; 367 (tl) O'Brien Productions/Corbis; (tr) Hughes Martin/Corbis; (br) Bob Rowan; Progressive Image/Corbis; (br) Royalty-free/Corbis; Page 387(t), 387(c), Harcourt Index; 387(b), Tom Stewart/Corbis; 388, 389(t), Harcourt Index; 389(b), Superstock; 390(t), 390(b), 391(t), 391(b), Harcourt Index; 392(t), Dave G. Houser/Corbis 392(c), Harcourt Index; 392(b), Ed Bock/Corbis; 393(t), Richard Hutchings/ Corbis; 393(c), Comstock.com; 393(b), Harcourt Index; 394(t), Harcourt Telescope; 394(b), 395(t), Harcourt Index; 395(b), Harcourt Telescope; 396(t), 396(b), Harcourt Index.

Illustration Credits

Mary Thelen, 14-15; Rosario Valderrama, 16-17; Keith Baker, 20-37; Loreen Leedy, 50-63; David Slonim, 72-81; John Kanzler, 82-83; David Sim, 84-85; Joe Cepeda, 88-95; Miko Imai, 120-139; Jane Conteh-Morgan, 140-149; Catherine Bennet, 149; Fabricio Vanden Broeck, 150-151; Martin Matje, 152-153; Silver Editions, 164-168; Rosalind Beardshaw, 184-201; Polly Powell, 202-211; David Gordon, 212-213; Marc Mongeau, 214-215; Arnold Lobel, 226-239; Mark Schroder, 243; Yuyi Morales, 248-255; Vitali Konstantinov, 256-263; Claudia Hammer, 264-265; Dagmar Fehlau, 266-267; Lea Daniel, 288-293; Jane Chapman, 296-317; Julie Carpenter, 318-327; Ilja Bereznickas, 327; Marc Mongeau, 328-329; Cindy Revell, 330-331; Silver Editions, 338-339; Steve Semour, 358-363; Maria Fernanda Oliver 368-375; Gerardo Suzan, 376-385; Jennifer Herbert, 387-396.